Soulwork 101

A New Age Guide to Personal Transformation

By

Glenn Stewart Coles

To: Sandra
Be Inspired!
Glenn

Order this book online at www.trafford.com
or email orders@trafford.com

Most Trafford titles are also available at major online book retailers.

Note for Librarians: A cataloguing record for this book is available from Library
and Archives Canada at www.collectionscanada.ca/amicus/index-e.html

Printed in Victoria, BC, Canada.

ISBN: 978-1-4251-8992-1 (Soft)
ISBN: 978-1-4251-8994-5 (e-book)

*We at Trafford believe that it is the responsibility of us all, as both individuals
and corporations, to make choices that are environmentally and socially sound.
You, in turn, are supporting this responsible conduct each time you purchase a
Trafford book, or make use of our publishing services. To find out how you are
helping, please visit www.trafford.com/responsiblepublishing.html*

*Our mission is to efficiently provide the world's finest, most comprehensive
book publishing service, enabling every author to experience success.
To find out how to publish your book, your way, and have it available
worldwide, visit us online at www.trafford.com*

Rev. date 06/01/2009

 www.trafford.com

North America & international
toll-free: 1 888 232 4444 (USA & Canada)
phone: 250 383 6864 ♦ fax: 250 383 6804 ♦ email: info@trafford.com

The United Kingdom & Europe
phone: +44 (0)1865 487 395 ♦ local rate: 0845 230 9601
facsimile: +44 (0)1865 481 507 ♦ email: info.uk@trafford.com

10 9 8 7 6 5 4 3 2 1

Table of Contents

THERE ARE MANY people who have influenced the creation of my unique perceptions. In particular, my father Stewart, mother Dorothy and sister Dianne helped shape me and provided incredible support at all levels. My mother Dorothy along with Dan Lauzon and Anita Ramo were my editors and I thank them for their insights. My fairy-friend Tunde provided tremendous spiritual guidance; she also opened connections to a new realm of spiritual friends. There are many other friends, family and mentors whom I love and thank, including Bob for his inspiration and Alan Parsons who asked me to put his name in my book.

Glenn Stewart Coles
December, 2008

As you read this book and do the exercises, you will be transformed; unless you choose not to transform.

As you transform, you begin to understand and apply the skills for changing your world.

The rest is up to you.

Are you ready to begin?

Introduction

WHOEVER READS THIS book with the intention of personal transformation will be changed.

You are who you think you are.

Any changes that you experience are entirely of your own creation. You are in charge each step of the way. For some the journey may be difficult, while others may awaken to new concepts with joy and pleasure. The journey is wondrous, the path is fresh, and the universe is unlimited.

You will discover that all change comes from within. You will also discover that a deeper understanding of self can assist in the creation of a new future. Your perceptions play a key role in every experience that you have. Becoming aware of perceptions is an important step in activating personal change.

What is Transformation? Ultimately, transformation will be what you define it to be. For some the changes will be great and for others they will be minor. In either case, the most important aspect is the perceived value of the changes and the resulting lifestyle experiences that are generated by the new you. When you live with joy, the world feels different.

You may wish to benchmark your own transformation. Begin by documenting your current feelings about who you are and who you want to be. Take a good deep look at yourself and begin to identify those aspects in your life that hold you back. Also pay focused attention on activities that propel you forward. You may wish to set measurable goals prior to beginning a transformational phase, but these will be your own measurements based on what matters to you.

In order to change our experiences and outcomes in life, it is necessary to change 'who you are'. You will discover that there are many aspects of self that you are quite content with. The task becomes to identify and alter the vibrations that keep you from being what you want to be. When you finally get there, you will realize that you have simply changed your state of being. You are in charge of yourself, and every potential is possible.

Whatever you are comes from within. No matter what brought you to where you are today, you are what you are. You may be very pleased with many things about yourself, or very disappointed. You may have accepted that survival is the most important thing and do what you have to do. You may take your survival for granted. You may have a support network, or you may be alone. No matter what led you to be who you are today; everything that defines you comes from within.

You continue your journey with the next step...

Transformation

'You are the world.
When you transform yourself, the world
you live in will also be transformed.'

Deepak Chopra, 'The Way of the Wizard', 1995

Transformation of Self

The intention of this book is to help you grow·

You may discover throughout this journey that personal growth is not an accumulation of things but an accumulation of understanding, happiness, and comfort with oneself. The transformation of self is something that only you can do. Your reading of this book indicates that you are ready for change.

This book provides concepts, suggestions and guidelines intended to stimulate thought that may help you define yourself and your personal philosophy. You will also be presented with some brand new ideas. What you change and how you change will be left up to you. You decide who you are and who you want to be. You may also discover elements of yourself and your character that you are perfectly comfortable with, and have no desire to change. That is okay, as you are the creator of your own experience.

You will discover that personal change
can be both simple and complex·

Sometimes change requires planning and effort over time, while in other cases change occurs immediately upon the realization of a new concept. Change can also occur gradually and easily by gaining new perception and persistently pointing yourself in the desired direction.

There are many ways to work with this book·

You could read it through from beginning to end. You could jump around to the sections or chapters that interest you. You could keep a journal of your self-discovery, answering the questions at the end of each chapter. You could even join or form a discussion group, working though the exercises together. Whatever method you choose, your transformation is up to you. As you read the book, you may discover that some change takes place naturally while other alterations require deeper thought and dedication.

This is your journey and you choose the mode of transportation·

You may find that it is necessary to re-read a section numerous times before you understand and digest the information. You may also choose to assist your transformation by purposely keeping the concepts high in your mind. At the end of each section, there are Transformational Questions intended to trigger your thoughts. Resolve to have an answer to these questions prior to reading the next chapter. You may wish to write your response in detail, to incorporate the questions into a discussion group, or to simply think things through in depth. You may even decide to let your dreams or meditations provide you with answers.

Be aware of your own resistance to certain topics·

If you are not answering a question because it makes you feel uncomfortable, then perhaps it is even more important to answer the question. If you feel an emotional charge when you think about a certain question, consider this a signal light for an area requiring investigation. Part of personal transformation involves identifying and understanding your own barriers. On occasion these barriers may be challenging.

Achieve a comfort level with your own beliefs and path·

Sometimes the concepts will feel familiar and comfortable to you, while in other cases the concepts will be entirely new. In some cases, you will agree completely with the presentation, while other articles may awaken objections. Diversity is one blessing of our existence and you are entitled to your own opinions. What is important is for you to gain a new understanding of yourself and to achieve a comfort level with your own beliefs and life path.

The path of transformation may not always be easy·

You may have thoughts that you cannot succeed. There may be many aspects of self that are ingrained and painful to address. Some people may face more challenges than others. However, there is no journey that you are incapable of taking. Never forget that you are unique, that your journey is unique, and that you choose your own path.

May you experience peace, joy, fulfillment, and enlightenment as you gain a greater understanding of your existence.

Transformational Exercises

1. Make a list of the elements of your life that you would like to change.

2. Make a list of characteristics that you prefer to keep.

3. Are there any characteristics that conflict with your ability to change?

Mirror, Mirror

WHEN WAS THE last time that you looked at yourself in the mirror?

Perhaps you were getting ready to go out, and were checking your appearance for potential corrections. Perhaps you brushed your hair, or fixed your makeup, or straightened your tie. When you walked away, were you satisfied with your appearance, or did you carry doubts with you?

Some people look in the mirror and project self-judgment. We look at our physical appearance in more detail than anyone else would. We may see things that we don't like and focus on imperfections. Some people have difficulty looking straight into their own eyes and their personal level of self-esteem becomes evident.

A friend of mine taught me to have discussions with 'the man in the mirror'. He describes it as 'talking to the smartest person I know'. It may sound strange, but it is very interesting to experience. Have a discussion with the face in the mirror. Ask a question or offer advice and see what happens.

Can you look at your reflection in the mirror and feel only love and appreciation? Tell yourself that you are perfect and believe it. Tell yourself that everything is okay, that you are doing well in life, and that you are a wonderful person. If you feel any resistance as you make these statements, ask yourself why.

The next time that you look in the mirror, overlook the surface of your physical appearance. Eliminate all thoughts about your past and future and exist in one solitary moment. Take a good long look at the bright and glowing soul shining back at you and recognize your inner light.

Transformation Exercises

1. Find a mirror in a private place during a private time and really look at yourself.

2. Understand which elements of self you would like to change.

3. Try to see past all judgment and realize the joy of your soul.

4. Write down descriptions of any feelings that were awakened by these exercises.

How to Change Your Life

MOST OF THE activities in our life are a series of repetitive tasks. Look at what you do every day and realize that you are repeating the same things over and over again. Specific tasks may change on a daily basis, but if you look at them over a week they remain constant. From laundry and cleaning to eating and personal hygiene, the general activities we undertake define the life that we lead.

Our thoughts can follow the same pattern as our actions. Every day, most of our thoughts are the same as yesterday. In particular, thoughts that cause us anguish and despair tend to surface regularly. We find ourselves in a rut, unable to stop thinking about things that have gone wrong, or desires that are unfulfilled.

Understanding the repetitive nature of our life, it is easy to see how we can fail to progress. If the things that you think about regularly are not guiding you towards an ideal, then they tend to keep you where you are. Often, we create the very things that we wish to avoid. If you are not happy with your current situation, is it any wonder that staying in the same frame of mind can become tedious and depressing?

How does one begin the process of change? It is easy to identify the habits and thoughts that rule your life. However, when we try to change we find ourselves falling back habitually into the same repetitive actions and thoughts. It is almost like playing back a video and hoping that the movie has a different ending.

It is important to focus not on changing the old but creating the new.

Design your new life and then live by it. Choose something that you are going to do every day and then do it. Make it your utmost priority to repeat the same action daily and suddenly you will find that your chosen activity has become part of your life. Whether your self-improvement is on a physical, emotional, mental or spiritual level, adding positive activities to your daily routine assists in changing your environment.

In the science of psychology, there is a practice called behavioral modification. Based on the theory that all behavior is learned, the patterns that we follow are the result of either reward or internal conflict. Some behavior is the response to stimuli, a regular reaction that we experience following a common event. Other behavior is based upon expectation of consequence. Some consequences are good, resulting in reinforcement of the behavior. Other consequences are undesirable, resulting in avoidance of a certain behavior or replacement with action that removes the negative consequence.

Self-modification of behavioral patterns works best when we learn and reinforce new behaviors rather than suppressing or punishing unwanted ones. By focusing our energy on what we want to be, instead of what we don't want to be, we allow ourselves to move into the new pattern. By changing the stimuli, or by altering the consequences, we can train ourselves to look and live in a new direction.

The first step in modifying your own behavior is to gather baseline data. Observe and understand your current behavioral patterns before beginning any adjustments. The stage of awareness and recording assists transformation in two ways. Firstly, it provides a pattern for comparative measurement. Without knowing your own behavior in detail, how can you identify if any change has taken place? Secondly, the act of creating a baseline makes us more observant of our behavior and may help identify root causes. Knowing the root of your issues can make it much easier to correct them.

Are there things in your life that you want to change? Begin to identify them, and document the behavior that causes the undesired outcome. Choose to take the first step towards changing your self and your life.

Transformation Exercises

1. Carry a notebook for few days, and list everything that you do. Pay attention to your physical actions, what you ingest, how you feel, what you say, and how you react to situations.

2. As your lists progress, identify repetitive behavior.

3. Identify personal habits that you like.

4. Identify personal habits that you would like to alter.

Can You Trust Your Senses?

ALL SCIENTIFIC OBSERVATIONS, and many of the decisions we make in life are based upon the information we get from our senses. We depend upon sight, hearing, taste, touch and smell to survive. However, as we examine our senses and how we influence them, we discover that there is more going on than simple observation.

We tend to trust sight more than other senses. 'What you see is what you get.' 'I saw it with my own eyes.' 'Seeing is believing.' Yet when a crowd of witnesses is asked to describe a crime or an accident, things begin to change. One person saw a brown car hit a blue car, while another saw a black car hit a green car.

Our version of what we see is based upon our beliefs, our attention, and our perceptions. We rarely see all that is occurring around us. Instead we fill in the blanks with assumptions. When asked to describe the furniture in a living room, we assume there was a couch there, even if we didn't see one. When we see something on a regular basis, we often overlook the details. Try to identify the eye color of a co-worker (or a close friend!) without checking before you answer.

Hearing is often based on assumptions. Have you ever heard a cat cry outside and thought it was a baby? Have you misheard what someone said, even when they were talking clearly? Have you failed to notice a loud repetitive sound until someone points it out? We are constantly surrounded by sound and learn to filter out much of the environmental noise that we are exposed to. Even when we tune in, our attention is focused on areas of interest. In a crowd, there may be many conversations going on, yet we listen only to the ones that interest us.

Taste is a sense that is ruled by personal experience. We have emotional ties to food and judge flavors based upon our expectations. For every food you can imagine, there are some people that love the taste and others that hate it. Who is right? Obviously, taste can only be measured on a personal basis. Even then, we make mistakes. Our sense of taste is influenced by sight and smell. Cover your nose and eat in the dark and even your favorite foods may taste bland.

Like taste, smell is based on experience. True, there are some smells that most people find unfavorable. However, when exposed to an odor continuously, we can learn to mask or ignore the scent. A person walking into a freshly painted house is very aware of the toxic fumes, while the painters don't even notice them. Perfume can smell wonderful or terrible, influenced by your attraction to the person wearing it. Though we can identify the slightest amount of a distinct odor in the air, such as when a neighbor starts the barbecue, we can completely overlook the odor of smoke on our clothes.

Our sense of touch is often influenced by subjective comparison. We define what we feel as hot or cold, hard or soft, nice or not nice. Touch can also be fooled through suggestion. I remember playing a game as a child in which I was blindfolded and my finger was pushed into a lukewarm orange. I was told that I was feeling an eye-socket, and I believed it until the blindfold was removed.

When you walk down the street, pay attention to where your senses are focused. Instead of just moving and thinking like most people, pay attention to everything. What do you choose to look at, and how do your feelings influence the interpretation of what you see? When you see a beggar on the street, do you feel love, compassion, anger, pity, hatred, fear or apathy? Or did you even notice him? Stop for a moment, close your eyes, and listen to all the sounds around you.

All sensory input is an interpretation of your environment, based not only on observation, but also on training, expectations, experiences, and judgment. Focusing your attention is a choice you make so that you receive the input that you desire. Since each person has a different background and may make different choices, we cannot be sure that our senses are telling us the complete story. Perception of anything is not necessarily true.

Transformation Exercises

1. In the room you are sitting, become aware of the input from each of your senses.

2. Take a walk, and pay extra attention to what you see, hear, taste, smell, and touch.

3. How has previous experience or training affected what you saw, heard, tasted, smelled, or felt?

What is Reality?

PARENTS OFTEN HAVE a difficult time explaining reality to children. Patch Adams is real, but Marcus Welby isn't. Princess Diana was real, but Snow White isn't. The Dalai Lama is real, but Tom Sawyer isn't. Sometimes fiction is more believable than reality, yet we are required to know the difference.

Our definition of reality is based upon our five senses. That which we can see, hear, feel, touch and taste is recognized as real. Anything we cannot prove is seen as unreal. While we may have faith in intangible concepts such as God or reincarnation, we are aware of the distinction between reality and philosophy. Our understanding of reality is the root of our survival. We see dangers to avoid, hear sudden sounds, taste and smell food to determine if it is good or bad. Our senses help keep us alive.

The reality of our world operates by rules. The rules of gravity, space and time are insurmountable. Our bodies have limitations of strength and speed and aging and disease. We expect that these rules are true, so they are. Our core beliefs are set so deep that they happen automatically. If we step off a ledge, we don't have to think about falling, we simply do.

Do your remember your dreams? Within your dream world, there are no rules. As your physical body lies in a subconscious state, your mind travels through worlds created by your own vision. Scenes change quickly, from one place to the next. People undergo metamorphosis; an old friend turns into your grandmother; a rabbit talks; a sandwich runs away. Time is irrelevant, as travel can take place instantaneously.

We have different experiences in our dream world. In some dreams, we are the audience, watching events unfold. In others, we have direct control over occurrences. Lucid dreaming occurs when you identify being in the dream state while remaining asleep. We often wake up in bed and realize that we have been dreaming. What if you were to wake up inside a dream, recognize that you were dreaming, and remain asleep? In a lucid dream, there are no rules except the ones that you choose. In a dream, people can fly, animals can talk and food can run.

There are many reported occurrences of astral travel and out of body experiences. These are simply the next step of a lucid dream, moving into a state of transience without having to fall asleep. Consciously deciding to shut down and escape the physical body, you are now in a world of your making. Overcome your fears, clear your mind, ignore the rules, and simply create.

Do we choose to blindly accept the status of our being? What is reality? Is it the same for everyone? Individual perception plays a key role. One person sees a cat and feels love and compassion; another sees a cat and feels repulsion and fear. The cat has not changed, only the viewpoint. Group perception is also of tremendous importance, as we tend to believe what everyone else believes. Your personal belief in reality defines the life that you lead.

The lines of reality are not as clear as they may appear. What seems impossible is often a construct of training. From childhood on, we have formed a definition of reality based on both experience and input. However, it is possible to overcome training and find a way to change reality. A hundred years ago, it was unrealistic to imagine people flying in machines, instant communication around the world, or fixing someone's eyes with a burning hot light. What potential exists for us if we can only unlearn the rules?

Perhaps such concepts as telepathy, instant transportation, immortality, and metamorphosis are all possible. If we unlearn the bonds that keep us at this level, we could move onto the next. Experimentation with lucid dreaming allows the formation of new beliefs in a system without rules.

What are the constructs of your world? What holds you back, keeps you from progressing, brings you sadness or depression or defeat? Start to analyze the beliefs that hold you back, and decide if you want to keep them. Your reality is within your control.

Transformation Exercises

1. List five perceived realities that influence your life.

2. Describe how each reality has enhanced your life.

3. Describe how each reality has held you back.

4. Describe someone who did not abide by each of your rules of reality.

Living in the Moment

AN IMPORTANT QUESTION to ask yourself is 'does my mind rule me, or do I rule my mind?' Many people are constantly thinking, and these thoughts dominate their day. Whether the thoughts are analytical or emotional, we tend to get caught in thought loops. Once a thought becomes repetitive, it becomes habitual. Learning how to take charge of your thoughts is an important step towards self-management, and one of the key elements in meditation.

I am going to ask you to do something different. Get comfortable and prepare to read this chapter slowly, or perhaps someone could read it out loud. Learning of these skills involves participation and practice.

You are going to increase your awareness of your mind and how it works. Though we often don't apply the discipline, we are directly in control of our thoughts. By choosing where to focus our awareness, we can affect our environment and our emotions. I call this process 'checking in'.

Begin by evaluating yourself at this very moment. How do you feel? Is your posture comfortable? Sit in a position where both feet are placed on the floor. Much of your balance depends on being properly grounded. Having both feet on the floor also has the effect of straightening your posture.

Make sure that your spine is straight and your shoulders back. Much of the back pain and shoulder tension we experience is enhanced by bad posture, and we can begin to alleviate that tension just by changing position. As you read this sentence, align your body into a comfortable position. Sit straight and proud, and be aware of how your body feels. Is it different from moments ago?

Become aware of your breath. Try to breath only through your nostrils. Take in a deep breath to the count of four, and then hold for two seconds. Exhale slowly, again to the count of four, and again hold for two seconds. Repeat the process.

As you breathe, be aware of how you feel when you breathe in and

17

out slowly. Do you find it relaxing? The more that you practice this breathing technique, the deeper you will breathe. Try to completely fill your lungs with fresh life-giving oxygen. For a few moments, close your eyes and focus on your breathing.

Without moving, determine how each part of your body feels. Begin by identifying which area of your body carries the most tension. Is it your shoulders, your jaw, your stomach? Check in with your body and determine its current state.

Now begin to focus your awareness on various parts of your body. Start with your feet. How do they feel right at this moment? Wiggle your toes and get the blood circulating. If you are wearing shoes, you may want to take them off for the remainder of this article. Shoes bind our feet and separate them from the ground.

Next, move your attention to your legs. Become aware of your shins, your knees, your thighs. Can you feel the material of your clothing? Lift your toes off the ground and feel how the muscles tense in your legs. Push down with your feet and feel how your thighs tense up.

Now proceed to your torso. Are your stomach muscles tense? Take a couple of deep breaths and allow your stomach to expand. It's okay; no one is looking. Become aware of the feeling within your stomach area. Does everything feel in balance, or does your increased awareness identify any areas that may require attention.

Rest your palms on your stomach, and press the heels of your hands into your sides. Give your stomach a light massage, starting just below the rib cage and continuing to the waist. This area is known as the hara, and contains most of the body's vital organs. Regular massage in this area is very health inducing.

The area where many people carry their tension is in the neck and shoulders. Slowly bend your head forward and stretch your neck. Reach back and rub your muscles where there is tension. If there is a lot of tension, squeeze your fingers into the muscle and help it relax. Then, while sitting or standing, raise your shoulders in a shrugging position, and then allow your shoulders to drop. Do this two or three times.

Now move your awareness to your head. Focus on the muscles of your face and allow any tension to dissipate. Your mouth should be closed as you breath through your nostrils, but your teeth should be apart within your mouth. Relax your jaw.

While you have been reading this article, I have asked you to focus your awareness on various aspects of your physical being. This required you to live only in the moment. Any thoughts that were not directly in line with the text were thoughts created by you. Did you feel anxiety when you focused on certain areas? Did your concentration wane as you thought about what else you had to do? Was your mind occupied with worries?

Living for the moment involves stopping the mind chatter. Unless you are in a crisis situation, postponing worries for ten minutes makes things better, not worse. Learning how to manage your thoughts can change your life. Free your mind for a few moments each day, and begin to appreciate yourself and your surroundings.

Transformation Exercises

1. How did you feel before doing the routine?

2. Follow the routine exactly as described.

3. How do you feel after doing the routine?

4. Which parts were easy, and which parts were difficult?

5. Set an alarm clock or timer for twenty minutes. When the timer goes off, 'check in' with yourself and write down how you feel. Do this a few times in a row.

6. Practice 'checking in' every day and learn how to stop mind chatter.

Connections

OUR LIFE IS affected by other people. With each interaction, different aspects of self are magnified. Perhaps you can think of people in your life who make you laugh, or make you sad, or make you angry. Perhaps there are people that frequently stimulate certain feelings, either positive or negative. We tend to associate others with our feelings and will often anticipate an interaction before it happens.

If you can manage to step back and observe your interactions, you discover that all feelings are created internally. While someone else may act as a stimulus (even aggressively), our reactions always come from within. This is much more noticeable when you meet many people that you do not know well. Since we attach strong feelings to our long-term and close relationships, observing our own behavior with strangers allows us to bypass emotional attachments and simply observe personal reactions.

Many times, we project our feelings and beliefs on others. When we meet someone new, judgments can form quickly based on cultural training and biases. By looking rather than listening, we overlook the soul of the newcomer and instead create our own story about who they are and what they want from us. We tend to project expectations and then recognize feedback that supports our expectations.

When someone talks about an issue that disturbs us, we can learn by focusing more on the issue than the person. Why is it that a particular topic generates feelings within us? Why can thoughts of a person change our mood, even when they are not present? What is going on inside that you need to be aware of?

If we recognize how external input creates reactions, we begin to understand the connections within ourselves. When we become aware of responses from within, we have a deeper understanding of self. Once our responses become evident, the element of choice enters. Awareness allows choice, and choice allows us to direct our future according to our desires.

Consider the possibility that every person enters your life for a reason. The reason may be a growth opportunity for you, it may be of benefit to the other, or it may be a combination of both. Every interaction of souls can have a positive, negative or neutral effect, and the outcome has as much to do with you as it does with the other person.

Our connections to others are strong and exist to support and enhance our desires. There are also many connections within, including triggers that influence your reactions and behavior. Awareness of these connections can help you create the world that you desire.

Transformation Exercises

1. List five people who awaken emotions; someone who makes you smile, feel angry, feel irritated, feel respectful, and feel protective.

2. Make another list, with five new names, and match them to the same emotions.

3. What does each pair have in common?

The Transformation Game

I was recently playing a board game called 'The Transformation Game', in which players proceed through physical, emotional, mental and spiritual levels by gaining Life Insights and overcoming Life Setbacks. Along the way, Life Angels help out, offering enlightenment in various ways. As various cards are chosen from a deck, keywords are offered with the intention of awakening personal understanding about self and situation.

At one point, I drew four cards in a row. The words presented were 'focus, awareness, inspiration, and knowledge'. By the end of the game, these four words had helped me gain a clear understanding of my situation. In order to see the signs that come to us continuously, we must be open to accepting messages. Sometimes messages have meaning simply because we give them meaning.

In the process of manifestation, thoughts become words become actions become manifest. We create according to our thoughts, sometimes unconsciously or unintentionally. If we look deeply at any situation in our lives, we can usually identify elements of our own participation in its creation. Though we may not be directly to blame, or deny any intention for certain outcomes, our experiences have led each of us to where we are today. We can always look in retrospect to gain better understanding of cause and effect in our lives.

The prime directive of manifestation is focus. In order to create a desired future, one must continually move in the direction of that future. There may be differences between the path and your expectations, but the key is to adjust and keep moving towards a goal. When your attention wavers and focus shifts to another topic or intention, progress towards the original goal may be halted or a setback may be suffered. Regain focus, and progress continues.

One can become too intent on a goal, and miss seeing the numerous opportunities presented by the universe. As said by Helen Keller, 'When one door of happiness closes, another opens; but often we look so long at the closed door that we do not see the one that has been opened for us.' Sometimes it helps to redefine goals as we progress. Once you have gained focus on your goal, it is time to expand your awareness. Look beyond what you see and begin to understand how the flow of energy leads towards the fulfillment of your goal.

As awareness grows, inspiration follows. Inspiration is divine knowledge, an understanding of how everything works, and how to create a universe that includes your desired outcomes. It is a moment of epiphany, a point of enlightenment in which everything makes sense.

The answers are around us, waiting to be seen. When we focus our attention towards the creation of desires, and expand our awareness to include a higher view of situations, we can experience moments of inspiration that lead to new understanding, and then gain the knowledge of universal perfection.

Transformation Exercises

1. Identify an important goal that you have already achieved.

2. What specific steps did you take to achieve that goal?

3. What coincidences occurred to help you achieve your goal?

4. What was your moment of inspiration, when you realized that the goal was achievable?

Fool on the Hill

An old man sat on top of a hill, searching for the meaning of life.

He gazed at the stars and felt small. In the dark sky there were millions and millions of tiny lights. Each light could be a sun possibly larger than ours. Around those suns could be planets, and on those planets could be life. Some of the points of light were entire galaxies containing millions of suns. The universe seemed to go on forever, a limitless space in each direction, farther than imagination.

At the corner of his eye one of the lights moved, and he turned his head to focus on the movement. It was not a star but a firefly, winking its taillight in search of a mate. The firefly flew close by, and he caught it in his hand. As the green harmonic glow radiated from the creature in his fist, he realized how big he was. To this tiny fly he was gargantuan, and yet there were still smaller creatures to which this fly would seem huge.

And then he realized that from his unique perspective, he was the center of the universe. He could imagine the expansion of the universe, getter larger forever. He could also imagine shrinking microscopically, and being able to see molecules, and then atoms, and then electrons. In both directions, the smallness and largeness never end.

It was then that it came to him. The absolute power of being in the center of the universe meant that the meaning of life could be whatever he wanted it to be. From that point, he was able to create anything, to set his thoughts and influence his world. *He realized that the meaning of life would not come from outside but from within.*

He stood to walk down the hill, happy and content.

He now knew the meaning of life, and knew that everything was fine.

Transformation Exercises

1. Do you believe that you have a purpose in life? What is it?

2. Do you feel that you are on track with your life path?

3. What alterations would you like to see in your everyday existence?

Values

'Open your arms to change, but don't let go of your values.'

Dalai Lama

The Franklin Process

THE EASIEST WAY to understand a person and the choices that they will make is to have a clear understanding of their values. Values are the driving force behind all decisions and actions, and lead someone along the life path of their choosing. Though personal values are influenced throughout life by parents, society and experiences, they tend to be formed early and remain constant.

In 1734, when he was 28 years old, Benjamin Franklin wrote a detailed letter to himself outlining the principles that would guide his life. Included in his list of thirteen values were such characteristics as humility, cleanliness, tranquility, justice and industry. Throughout his very productive life, Franklin continuously reviewed his values to ensure that he was on track with his higher desires. While he found some of them a challenge to maintain, there were others in which he succeeded gloriously.

In 1994, when I was 37 years old, I undertook the exercise now known as the Franklin Process. By identifying the values that were important to me, I not only set a path for my future, but also gained a new understanding of the choices that had led me to be who I am. Over the next few years, I continued to refine and expand my personal value statement, with the end result being The Millennium Prayer (next page). These are the values by which I choose to lead my life.

As you identify your own personal values, remember that specific values are not right or wrong. What is important to one person may seem trivial or in conflict with the values of another. That is okay. As long as one does not impose on the rights of another, a person can choose which values to give priority.

The most important thing about values is to be sure that they indicate the way you want to lead your life. To both learn about yourself and guide your future, take the time now to go through the Franklin Process, and create your own personal value statement.

Transformation Exercises

1. Create a list of values that you will consider for your value statement.

2. Choose the five values that are most important to you.

3. Define what these values mean to you.

4. Are you on track with each value?

5. Identify how each value has helped your progress.

6. Identify how each value has hindered your progress.

The Millennium Prayer

UNIVERSAL ENERGY, OF which I am part, I pledge to create a world of peace and joy.

I am tolerant of the values and beliefs of others and feel love and respect for all living creatures.
I accept that others worship their god in their own way.
I practice kindness, compassion, sincerity and honesty.
I help others when I can, through sharing, healing or charity.

I place myself neither above nor below any other being.
I listen to and understand what others are trying to say.
I learn from the elders and teach the youth.
I learn from the youth and teach the elders.
I recognize that I have something to learn from everyone and everything on the planet.

I care for my body, the temple of my existence.
I eat nutritional foods, exercise regularly, and maintain awareness of my physical state.
I care for my emotional state and enjoy peace of mind.
I fast regularly, for both physical and spiritual cleansing.
I meditate and increase my capabilities as a human.
I do not let my desires overcome my values.

I cherish my planet as a living entity.
I focus my efforts on healing the earth and its inhabitants.
I put great consideration into the creation of life.

I harm no one, either through intention or lack of action.
I control my anger and do not display it to others.
I find constructive ways to release energy.
I practice non-violence.
I will not carry a weapon.

I continuously seek learning, becoming well-educated, well-informed and inquisitive.
I am an explorer, a traveler and a creator.

I am optimistic, grateful and philosophical
I am enthusiastic, productive and adventurous.
I am moral, ethical and live life with integrity.

I am open to the guidance of synchronicity and do not let expectations hinder my path.
I find hope in the darkest of days and focus in the brightest.
I do not judge the universe.

Written by Glenn Stewart Coles, 1999.

After All, We're All the Same

ONE OF THE most evident contrasts in our lives is that of male/female. Based on cultural stereotypes, women tend to be more verbal, more nurturing, and more expressive. Men tend to be more logical, aggressive, and visual.

When a woman is aggressive, she is said to be showing her 'masculine' characteristics. Similarly, a man who is loving and caring, or (god forbid) cries, is said to be feminine. Many men feel threatened when another man shows his feminine side. Often seen as weakness, men who are not hormonally dominated face derision and laughter. Women displaying their masculine side face the same prejudice. When we do not fit into the roles defined by society, we risk judgment by others.

Our gender identity develops from a young age. One of the first questions asked after a birth is 'boy or girl?' From that moment our impressions and treatment of the child are dependent on gender. A baby boy is treated differently than a baby girl. He is tossed into the air, while she is stroked lovingly. He gets toy trucks and tools and guns, she gets dolls and Easy Bake Ovens™. Our roles in society are defined by culture, media, family and friends.

The training continues as a child grows up. Girls are supposed to be nice and pretty and to act like a 'little lady', carrying sugar and spice and everything nice. Boys are supposed to be strong and tough and to 'act like a man', with pockets full of strings and nails and puppy-dog tails. Variance from the norm results in feedback to the child, who realizes that he/she has done something wrong. We adjust our behavior based on the approval factor.

As we reach our teenage years, the gender difference becomes even more prominent. Girls begin to grow breasts and boys begin to stare at them. Attractive females get more attention than they want and learn to avert their eyes so as not to encourage strangers. Females deemed less attractive by social standards learn that people treat them differently and may devalue their self-worth.

Boys begin to mature, and learn the benefits of physical prowess. Those who are stronger and faster are also better liked. Boys who are weak or fat or slow are picked on. In male society, value is often determined by athletic ability. Even though intelligence, kindness and the ability to communicate are critical aspects of character, it is the quarterback who gets all the dates.

By the time we reach adulthood, the concept of gender is permanently set into our ego. We identify ourselves as male or female. Actions and behaviors related to our gender are evident. We act and talk differently with the opposite sex than we do with our own. Our body, our mind, our beliefs and our actions are affected by the gender-identity that we have developed.

A few years ago, I was speaking with a friend about past lives. She revealed a memory of a life as a sailor who had drowned when the ship sank. The discussion gave me a revelation. In the days when wooden ships crossed the oceans, all sailors were men. Her memory of a previous life was as a man. Then it struck me.

The soul has no gender·

Our soul, the essence of our existence, is that which carries on after our physical life concludes. Our life force, contained in our body, does not carry with it a gender identity. That which makes us human only begins to realize gender through physical attributes, social interaction and training. Deep down, we are all the same.

The next time you find yourself classifying and judging someone by their sexual identity, understand that beyond the physical, we are all equal. Speak to the soul and you will realize a new perception.

Transformation Exercises

1. List your dominant gender characteristics.

2. What aspects of the opposite gender are parts of your character?

3. Choose a male and female role model, and describe their gender characteristics.

4. How do you speak or act differently with men and women?

Life Matters

THE OTHER DAY, my cat caught a dragonfly. Leaping into the air, she caught the insect in mid-flight with a display of reflex and physical prowess. She brought it inside the house alive and buzzing. For the next few minutes, she played a game with the insect, letting it get away and then pouncing on it. For a cat, the pleasure comes not from the kill but from the capture. During the game, the dragonfly managed to escape and hide underneath a heat vent. I knew that its death was merely postponed, as cats have incredible patience.

Then a thought crossed my mind. If this were a bird that the cat was tormenting, I would rescue it. Why would I consider a dragonfly not worthy of my compassion? Is it of less value than a bird simply because it is an insect? I got up from my vantage point and reached into the heat vent, gently grabbing the bug. I took it outside and let it go. Despite the bashing by the cat, it was well able to fly away.

A couple of days later, my values were tested again when I saw another cat with a bird in its mouth. At first the bird hung lifeless from the cat's jaws, then it started to flap its wings. It escaped momentarily, only to be smacked with a paw and picked up again. Its head was fully inside the cat's mouth, and I knew that if I did not intercede the torment would continue for a while until the cat got bored. Then the deathblow would be struck.

I went over to the cat, picked it up and pulled open its jaws. The bird, which had been feigning death, suddenly flew away. The cat scratched me for my intrusion, and ran after the bird. It was too late and the bird flew to safety. I had rescued another creature.

Some people may think it is silly to care so much about creatures of little worth. Birds don't think, insects don't feel, and cats kill things naturally. It is the circle of life, and there is nothing that I can do about it. Why waste my time?

Then I read about cruelty to animals in the newspaper. Is there something wrong with me for feeling displeasure in watching a creature suffer? Is saving a dragonfly a silly effort? Or is it others who are wrong, the people who believe that life is inconsequential? I know that there are many atrocities in this world that are a lot worse than maiming a kitten. Where do we draw the line in determining which creatures are worthy of compassion? If we believe that one creature is less worthy than another, is it a great leap to believe that one human is less worthy than another? How we treat other life forms is a statement of our own level of humanity.

I know that there are animals that have died to keep me alive. I do eat meat, and I do wear leather. I hope and rationalize that the animal was killed humanely, and thank it for giving its skin and flesh to support me. What I cannot accept is the senseless causing of pain or death. Any creature that lives wishes to survive, and though all living creatures eventually pass on, it is not right to make them suffer. Life matters.

Transformation Exercises

1. Describe an incident where you have killed a life form.

2. Describe an incident where you have saved a life.

3. Identify the feelings associated with each situation.

4. Do animals have a soul?

Two Brothers

Two BROTHERS LIVED in a house in the mountains. It was a beautiful house, built of wood, with lots of rooms. The view was spectacular. Covering the mountains were trees, tall and strong, reaching for the sky. Across the valley were other mountains, standing forever powerful. Animals and flowers grew abundantly.

One day, the brothers were in town doing errands when the rain began. It rained so hard that a bridge was washed out and the brothers could not get back home. They stayed in town for days, worried about their home. 'Oh, what can we do?' moaned the one brother, 'I hope that everything is okay'. 'We will find out in time, my brother,' replied the other. 'In the meantime, let us put our energy into doing what we can.'

Finally, the rains stopped and the bridge was rebuilt. The brothers returned to their home, and it was gone. A river of mud had washed down the mountain, demolishing the house. The trees remained, the view remained, but the house was gone.

'I am ruined,' said the first brother. 'Everything that I have done in my life so far has gone into that house; all of my possessions, all of my work, and all of my savings. Without the house I have nothing. I have nowhere to live and nowhere to go.'

The second brother stood silent for a while. Looking at the base of the mountain, he described what he saw: 'I see bricks and wood and pipes and shingles. A house is simply a building, and all material is immaterial. We are still alive and healthy, brother. My essence still exists. I am not my house.'

The brothers moved to the city and began to look for work. They were soon offered a job washing dishes. The first brother said 'I don't want to do that. We are better than that. What will people think of us if we become dishwashers?'

The second brother said 'I am not my job. I am unique and special, as are you. My job is simply where I choose to spend some of my time. In the meantime, let us put our energy into doing what we can.'

Over the years, the first brother mourned the loss of his house, and regretted his lot in life. He always knew that things could have been better and wondered what karma had brought his suffering to him.

The second brother took the job as a dishwasher and acquired a new home. He found joy in rising each morning and joy in laying down each night. He thanked the heavens for allowing him life in such a beautiful world.

After many years, the first brother died. All of the friends of the two brothers showed up, and declared how horrible it all was. 'How will you live without your brother? What will you do?' The remaining brother replied 'I am not my brother. I rejoice in the life that he led. I thank the heavens for allowing us so many years together. In the meantime, I will put my energy into doing what I can'.

Finally, the day arrived when the old man lay in his bed, living his last days. His loved ones crowded around the bed, grieving with sorrow. 'Why must you die?' they exclaimed. He replied, 'In a few moments, I will take my last breath. And as I exhale, remember that I am not my breath. My essence continues on.'

All suffering is caused by our attachment to the world and how we choose to perceive it. We become attached to material items, to places and environments, and to our body and the pleasures we experience. In a dynamic environment, nothing lasts forever. Remain attached to the material world and you will be disappointed. See your existence as a transient pleasure and joy awaits.

Transformation Exercises

1. What are your most valued possessions?

2. How would you feel if you had no material possessions?

3. If your house were on fire, what would you carry out?

Four Steps to Enlightenment

FOR SOME, LIFE is drudgery, filled with labor and duty, ending with nothing. We watch helplessly as the world crumbles around us, shaken by hate and violence and poverty. We overcome our sorrow with intoxicants and pleasures and possessions, hoping that the sadness does not affect us. We fail to realize that it already has.

Others see our planet glowing with energy, radiant with life, and capable of such happiness that we can barely contain it. There is beauty everywhere and we pride ourselves in being a part of the whole. Every moment of existence is bliss and we move forward with anticipation, creating wonders that are the envy of the universe.

You may have placed yourself in one group or the other, or perhaps somewhere in-between. What I tell you now is that each of us has the potential to create either of these realities. There is nothing that is impossible. You have much greater influence on the world than you imagine.

Though the four steps to enlightenment sound simple, our challenge is to incorporate these steps into every waking moment. Once you know the steps, remain aware of any circumstance when you stray from the path, and adjust accordingly. Attitude and perception are critical components, and once you fully realize that you are completely in control, following the steps becomes a matter of choice.

1. Accept everything as it is, including yourself.

The desire to change your environment causes frustration. In this very moment, realize that everything is as it should be, and that is good. Of course, you could come up with a list of things you would like to change, but for now all of that is irrelevant. Understand that the world around you, the people you know and don't know, and everything about yourself, is perfect. Accept that perhaps things are the way they are for reasons you don't yet understand.

2. Do not judge anything.

The existence of polarity causes us to create comparisons. Good and bad, black and white, hot and cold, male and female. We define our world by differences and our task is to realize that these differences are irrelevant. When you think of male and female, remember that the soul has no gender. When you think of hot and cold, remember that sunlight may feel warm in winter, and a breeze may feel cool in summer. When you think of good and bad, understand that these definitions are created by your own needs, morals, desires and perceptions.

3. See that everything is interconnected.

We tend to see ourselves as individuals and to define everything around us as separate. This is not true. We all breathe the same air, we all feel the same feelings, and we all share the same energy. Everything that you do affects everything else and vice versa. The qualities that you like or dislike in others are mirroring the qualities that you like or dislike about yourself. We are all one, and part of the singular energy that we call god, spirit, or the universe.

4. Manifest love in your heart.

It is easy to love something that you like. It is often difficult to love something that you don't like. Overcoming this challenge is a necessary step on the path to enlightenment. Loving everything and everyone cannot be just rational thought. It must become something that you feel. When you see someone that you judge or dislike, realize that they are just another soul on a journey, and feel love and thankfulness that they are the person that they are. To truly attain this goal, there can be no exceptions. Everyone deserves your love.

It is an important step to love everything about yourself as well. Despite what you may think, you are perfect and are exactly where you should be today and now. Nothing in your past matters and nothing in your future affects you yet. This very moment, you are a creature of beauty, perfection and love. When you begin to accept this, not just from a rational level but as something you feel from deep inside, you begin your path to enlightenment.

Transformation Exercises

1. Say the names of the four steps until you know them.

2. Which step do you think will be most difficult to achieve?

3. Throughout your day, make a list of perceived judgments.

4. Determine why these judgments may be incorrect.

Beliefs

'If you have a particular faith or religion, that is
good. But you can survive without it.'

DALAI LAMA

Lightworkers

THERE IS A new breed of human that is populating our species. We have been around for centuries, and again we are called. We are the same as everyone, and yet we are different. We have always recognized our uniqueness, and yet it is now that the lightworkers awaken.

It is not religious belief that defines light work; in fact there are many who create darkness in the name of their religion. Lightworkers do not all pray to the same god; in fact some pray to many gods while others pray to none. Light work involves faith beyond religion.

On the surface, light work is indicative of various human emotions and behaviors. Compassion, generosity, kindness, and nurturing are all ultimately the result of love. The lightworker helps rather than hinders, heals instead of harms. In fact, many lightworkers are already healers, and many are women.

The way of the lightworker is not easy, and yet it is through lightworkers that humanity realizes it's greatest hope. The lightworker has two goals: to bring light where there is dark and to continually improve one's self. As self becomes stronger and more balanced, the ability to carry the light is strengthened.

There are many things that are not defined for lightworkers. For example, though I carry certain moral and ethical beliefs, there are others whose beliefs are just as valid. There are also those who allow their moral beliefs to bring darkness into the world.

Therefore, moral belief alone cannot be the measurement of light work.

The world is changing, and there is a lot going on. In every corner of the globe there are lightworkers holding their balance and helping others move in a positive direction. Lightworkers bring love wherever they go, and their resonance has influence beyond their comprehension. Stand forth and carry the light! The world can be changed, and it begins with you.

Transformation Exercises

1. Do you consider yourself a lightworker? Why?

2. How has being a lightworker made your life more difficult?

3. How has being a lightworker made your life easier?

Soul Man

EVERY PERSON HAS a different opinion about our existence. Some believe in life after death, while others believe that existence simply stops. Some believe in a soul, others do not. Some believe in a pre-determined plan, and others that life is random. The beauty of our beliefs is that any theory could be correct. We choose the beliefs that give us the most comfort.

Though we are inundated with stories of near-death experiences, astral travel, spiritual encounters and psychic knowledge, the onus of scientific proof lies within the physical world. That which cannot be perceived through the senses, or which cannot be replicated, is determined not to exist. Limited by our physical reality, acceptance of the non-physical can only occur through faith. To put it simply, faith is choosing to believe in something without proof.

Faith affects our attitudes and behavior. Those who believe in karma or Judgment Day will often alter their actions based upon the projected outcome. Some people do not kill, not because it is judged to be immoral, but because of the fear of eternal punishment. Strangely enough, others do kill, believing in an eternal reward. Some people experience lives of material accumulation, hedonistic pleasure, or sunken depression, believing that there is no further existence beyond this singular dimension. Others lead humble lives of chastity and poverty, believing that reward comes in the afterlife.

I believe that I have an eternal soul. I believe that each person has a soul, and that all souls are equal, regardless of the persona projected. We are each human representations of an eternal energy. Every soul is capable of growth and contribution. Every soul is worthy of my respect. Though conscience and training guide my personal definition of right and wrong, it is not up to me to judge the lives of others.

I believe that I have had many lives before this one, and potentially many lives after. The persona of Glenn Stewart Coles is but one representation of the entity that is me. Throughout my existence, I have personally been male and female, black and white, rich and poor, young and old. Knowing that I may have existed in many forms makes it easier to accept others as they are. How can I denigrate another for being different, when I may have led that existence myself in another time and place?

Before birth, and after death, we exist as eternal energy, one with the universe. All knowing and all seeing, we realize that life as a physical being offers us perceptions, viewpoints, and experiences that we cannot fully appreciate as our spiritual self. How can one who is immortal feel the pressures of time? How can one who has everything experience lacking, or desire, or anticipation, or fulfillment? Our omnipotent selves cannot feel fear, or depression, or discovery, or excitement. Thus, in order to experience life in its fullest, we choose to come into existence in this physical plane.

Since the life we lead is but a segment of reality, we play the game at many levels. Sometimes, a challenging life serves our purpose better than a life of ease. Knowing that suffering is perception rather than circumstance, we place ourselves in situations that offer us the greatest growth, both spiritually and emotionally. What is it like to be a warrior, a peacemaker, a thief who is caught or a thief who is not?

Each time we return to physical life, we desire to try something different. Sometimes the differences are immense, other times minute, but we would never choose to relive a moment that has already past. There should be no regrets, as each choice leads us to experiences that we would otherwise not achieve. Sometimes what an individual perceives as an undesired milestone was actually of tremendous benefit, leading to discovery that only the crisis could reveal.

The benefit and beauty of this philosophy is that nothing really matters. As an eternal being with many chances to do it over again, the concepts of success or failure takes on different meanings. For me, success is measured by my progress in understanding of myself, and the contributions that I make to others. The ultimate achievement in life is to be of service to humanity. I just like to do it a different way each time I come back.

Transformation Exercises

1. Do you believe that you have a soul?

2. Where did this belief (or doubt) come from?

3. What are your thoughts on reincarnation?

4. Can you remember any past lives? Even if the memories aren't clear, who do you think you were?

Instant Karma

WHAT IS KARMA? "What goes around comes around." "You reap what you sow." "Pay the piper." "Cause and effect." "Every action has an equal and opposite reaction."

This is Karma·

Knowing that our experiences are based on our thoughts and actions is confirmation that we control the future. If you are mean to people, you will encounter mean people. If you are a loving person, you will also receive love. Do bad and you will experience bad; do good and you will experience good.

Modern religions take the belief in karma a step further. The religions that believe in a solitary God, such as Christianity, Judaism, and Islam, see the results of our actions evaluated on Judgment Day. At the end of your life (or at the end of the world) God will sit in judgment of you and your deeds. If you satisfy proscribed requirements, you will exist in bliss for eternity. Break the rules, and you will suffer.

Other religions, such as Buddhism, Hinduism, and Taoism, believe in reincarnation and the concept of karma. The karma collected by your soul does not show all of its influence in one lifetime. It carries over, attached to your individual self. You accumulate good or bad vibrations, which you carry on to your next life. Whatever you give will come back threefold (or tenfold, depending upon the mathematician).

The God-religions do not believe in reincarnation. After all, once you have reached heaven, why would you want to leave? The Self-religions do believe in reincarnation, as the solitary entity continues on from life to life. In both cases, the karma that you have collected during your life matters at the end.

So there we have it. According to the world's religions, the life force of each individual carries on after death. In some cases, we go to heaven, in other cases we come back to earth. In either case, there is continuance. In order to progress we must follow the rules and regulations of the religion, or more specifically the sect within the religion.

The rules often include basic qualities such as love and kindness. There are often exceptions that allow us to overlook these general traits. The rules also define specific dogmatic practices that must be followed without exception. Break certain rules and you will suffer.

Fear-based policies have dominated the belief system of mankind for most of our existence. There is nothing wrong with faith, or in having a belief system that encourages hope and compassion. There is something wrong with a system that motivates through fear. Religions were developed not only to give people hope but also to keep them under control. You had better act according to the rules, or you will regret it.

It is time for our species to stop living in fear. It is not necessary to do things solely to prevent punishment. Instead, do things because they feel good. You will be judged for your behavior, but it is yourself who must do the judging.

As we educate our young, we need to help them develop an enhanced conscience. Not a conscience based on fear, but a conscience based on love and compassion. There is karma. We create the life that we experience. Knowing that we can direct our pathway should be enough motivation to lead us in a direction of purity.

I do not look at karma with fear. I look at karma with understanding. I accept karma as part of my life and it brings me joy. I know that I am on the right path.

I do not think that I won't have challenges in my life. Of course I will, and so will you. Challenges help us to grow. However, we often create our own challenges and we do so to stimulate growth. What matters most is how we react to circumstances and stimuli.

The secret of karma is to live for the moment. This is instant karma. At this very moment, are you happy with yourself? If so, everything is all right, and there is nothing to worry about. If not, you must alter your life to enhance your comfort level. At every moment in your life, be aware of your satisfaction of the moment. This will help guide you towards a greater future.

Transformation Exercises

1. Define your god.

2. How important is religion to you today?

3. How has religion influenced your life?

4. How do you feel about death, sin, duty and worship?

5. What are your beliefs about after-life?

Live Like Lincoln

IMAGINE A HOLOGRAPHIC video game that was so real, you could actually live the life of Abraham Lincoln from birth to death. While you played the game, your sense of time would be altered, so that you perceived a lifetime. However, upon conclusion you would discover that it was really only a brief experience.

Would you choose to keep detailed information in your consciousness, so that you did not go to Ford's Theater on the night of April 14, 1865? Or would you choose to subconsciously maintain a vision of Lincoln's life purpose, while allowing yourself to experience the flavor of each moment? Would the game be more fun if you knew how to win, or if you kept the illusion that every moment was new and all potentials were possible.

Not everybody would decide to take the game to the same conclusion. Perhaps there are thousands of potential realities for Lincoln, with variant life paths resulting from different choices, and only one of those paths allows Lincoln to be the president of the Civil War victor. Or perhaps Lincoln was destined to become president, regardless of the choices that he made in his youth.

You could alter the outcome of the game by maintaining certain beliefs. What would happen if you played the Lincoln game, but decided to favor slavery? How would the timeline be changed? Perhaps the capital moves to Atlanta, slavery remains an acceptable part of our culture, and America becomes an ally of the Nazis to conquer Britain and Russia in the 1940's. Knowing that you are playing a game that can be repeated over and over, you may choose to experiment with different scenarios.

During each moment of Lincoln's life, he made decisions that moved him towards the destiny that is now in our history books. In the present day, Lincoln's life is carved in stone, and we already know the decisions that he made. Did he really experience a life of free choice, or was he unknowingly trapped on a life path that is now fixed in the universe?

53

Before he became president, Lincoln was quoted as saying 'All that I am, or hope to be, I owe to my angel mother.' In deferring responsibility for his life, perhaps he was admitting that his path was already pre-determined.

Transformation Exercises

1. Describe how your life is ruled by free choice.

2. Described how your life is pre-destined.

3. Describe what you want to create with the rest of your life.

Child of Destiny

WAS ABRAHAM LINCOLN destined to become America's most revered president? Was it his predetermined fate to die from an assassin's bullet? What about Mother Theresa, Princess Diana, John Lennon or Winston Churchill? Were their paths laid out in a universal plan that was blindly followed, or was each of them directly responsible for the outcome of their lives?

I was sitting around a campfire with some friends, and one of them asked me 'What is the difference between fate and destiny?' My immediate answer was that 'fate is the belief that you do not control your experiences, and destiny is what you create with your life'. My personal belief is that we have tremendous influence over our environment and ourselves. So much that occurs in my life can be traced back to action or inaction on my part. Even when it appears that someone else is directly responsible for the events in my life, through introspection I realize how I influenced their behavior.

However, what about the concept of soul purpose? I also believe that I am here to manifest a dream that has already taken place. All of my life has led me to where I am today, and as I move forward through time, I realize that my vision has already manifested in another dimension. The paradox of existence is that each choice we make alters our pathway, yet all potential outcomes already exist.

Perhaps there is no destiny. Perhaps great men and women became that way through persistence and effort. Or perhaps destiny has been predetermined and the illusion of time and choice exists simply to allow the soul to experience the flavor and drama of life. Every moment of each day, we make decisions that affect our path and experiences. By choosing the life purpose that feels right, we directly influence the outcome that will become known as our destiny.

Transformation Exercises

1. What is your life purpose?

2. How has your current situation been predestined?

3. Remember a difficult event from your past, and explain how it was necessary to your life purpose.

Seven Sins

THROUGH BOOKS, MOVIES, and religious education, many of us have been warned about committing the seven deadly sins. The sins are: pride, envy, anger, sloth, avarice, gluttony, and lust. Should you commit these sins, the penalties are harsh. Sinners can expect to be dismembered alive, dropped into cauldrons of boiling oil, forced to eat rats, or smothered in fire and brimstone. Sounds pretty horrible, doesn't it? Let us look at each of these sins in more detail.

Pride is the excessive belief in one's own abilities. I am guilty of this sin, as I take pride in all that I do. I believe that through my choices and actions, I direct my own future and experiences. I trust in the power of the universe, but I refuse to give away all responsibility for my life. Do we really want to teach our children to not take pride in themselves?

Envy is the desire for another's traits, status, abilities, or situation. Doesn't this drive us all? While jealousy can result in harmful feelings, I choose to envy those things that I wish to attain for myself. Enjoying the success of others, I create role models whom I emulate. Is there anyone who is not slightly envious of Tiger Woods or Bill Gates or Oprah Winfrey? How can we aspire for growth and progress without desiring success similar to others?

Anger can be a strong emotion, and dwelling on issues can hold us back from contentment. However, anger can also be the fuel that initiates change. If people always accept things as they are, we cannot progress as a species. Anger has changed laws, toppled dictatorships, imprisoned those who abused the weak, and forced large organizations to act responsibly. While anger has caused much pain and sorrow, it has also created much of the positive change in humanity.

Sloth is the avoidance of physical or spiritual work. Though people who choose to contribute less than others cannot expect to achieve the same rewards, is it really serious enough to be thrown into a snake pit for eternity? Who decides which work is acceptable? Is it really necessary for us to work 60, 70 or 80 hours a week? Perhaps we would be wiser to lead a life with a little more balance.

Avarice, also known as greed, is the excessive desire for wealth. Apparently, it is more holy to live in poverty. I do believe that greed can be taken to excess, by overlooking the well-being of others in order to achieve personal gain. I also believe that the universe is truly abundant and that there is more than enough for everyone to live comfortably. The desire for more is often the driving force behind creativity, effort, production, and work. Without a hint of avarice, we may all choose sloth.

Gluttony is an inordinate desire to consume more than we require. Is there anyone who has not had a second helping when they were already full, or who has not had a little too much to drink? The existence of buffets in our society directly panders to the human tendency of eating more food than necessary. While gluttony may affect our health, it hardly seems worthy of eternal torment.

Lust is an inordinate craving for the pleasures of the body. Apparently, it is not alright to feel all right. To desire sex, to enjoy a backrub, to lavish in a hot bath or to sleep on a comfortable mattress are all sins of pleasure. To lead a virtuous life, we are to deny ourselves anything that feels good, especially sex. While procreation is a necessity, sexual intimacy should never be initiated for love and joy. What hogwash.

I agree that excessive focus on any of the listed sins could lead to personal difficulty. Too much of anything pushes us out of balance, particularly when we allow our desires to overcome our values and compassion. However, it seems to me that there is a hidden agenda to the seven sins. Though the stated intention is to prevent an eternity of pain and damnation for the followers, the real reason may be control of the pious believer.

What are the hidden messages behind the seven sins? Believe that your personal successes are unimportant, do not desire what others have, don't get angry about unfairness, work hard but don't expect a lot of money, don't consume too much, and don't expect to feel good. Only contrived fear could make people actually follow these rules.

Before any believers get upset with what I have said, my main point is that there is always more than one way to look at any topic. In the meantime, enjoy your sins; they just may be good for you.

Transformational Exercises

1. Describe your religious training as a child or young adult.

2. What benefits has religious belief brought to you?

3. What fears and/or guilt stand out most for you?

4. How deeply does this training affect you today?

5. Are there aspects of your religion that you feel you would be better off without?

Satanic Verse

HE HAS BEEN called Mephistopheles, Beelzebub, Lucifer, and Satan. Lord of the underworld, prince of darkness, king of lies. This fallen angel is responsible for all evil, and to blame for all temptations that lead us astray. Ladies and gentlemen, meet the devil.

Different sects of Christian religion give various levels of power and credence to the devil. Jehovah Witnesses go so far as to say that Satan 'is a real person'. There is one common agreement – the devil is a powerful entity working against god to corrupt mankind. This red-faced demon, identified by horns and trident when ruling below, can take many shapes and forms on earth. Beware, as his only goal is to lead you to the depths of hell.

To me, the scariest thing about the devil is that some people believe in him. They lie awake at night, tormenting themselves with visions of hell, and swearing that the devil will not influence them. They put fear into the hearts of their children, whose nightmares are blamed not on the parents but on the devil himself. They do terrible deeds then say that 'the devil was within'.

The devil is a myth, created by man to invoke fear and shift responsibility. Supported by a legion of imps, sprites, and demons, Satan was created within religion not only to represent evil but also to be an instrument of control. If the devil is a real threat to the soul of man, then the church is necessary for protection.

Belief in the devil gives people the ability to blame an outside source for their own transgressions. I'm sorry that I cheated on our marriage, but the devil influenced me. I'm sorry that I stole money, but it was the devil's fault. I'm sorry that I murdered, but the devil was in me. How convenient it is to shift blame.

Life is simplified when you do not take responsibility for your actions. Whether you blame the devil, the government, an ethnic group, an age group, a specific person, or society in general, shifting blame reduces your own power and accountability. Somehow, giving away power seems right in situations where you need an excuse.

The only evil that truly exists is within the hearts of men and women. Every one of us has choice in all matters and circumstances. Once we identify the difference between right and wrong, there is no one else to blame if we choose the wrong path.

There are many things in life that we blame on external influences. Our health, our financial situation, our success, and even our actions can be easily explained as the result of something outside of our control. We find relief in shifting responsibility, as it means that we are left pristine, the victim of a power greater than ours. We break the rules and declare innocence. We look for miracles to change our life, and then mourn the results.

The reality is that we are completely in control of our life. Though we are each unique, and some paths appear easier than others, every one of us can take charge today. Even when things happen to us that are outside our influence, we still have power over our perception. What some may interpret as punishment and damnation, others recognize as both a challenge and a learning experience.

The only devil that exists is the one you create. If you let your actions betray your morals, then you let your desires overcome your character. If you let hate, bitterness, and apathy rule your life, then you have chosen misery. Instead, realize that you are the only one that determines your path and live with the results. The devil is simply a representation of personal tendencies that lead you away from joy, happiness, peace, and love.

Every person faces challenge and temptation. Knowing that our experiences are a direct result of our actions is power in itself. There is no evil entity lurking behind a corner, waiting to lead you astray. The power of good and the power of evil are both within you. Which path do you choose?

In closing, I apologize if this reading has offended your beliefs in any way.

The devil made me do it.

Transformation Exercises

1. Draw or describe a picture of the devil.

2. Where in your past did this image come from?

3. Do you feel that your power is within yourself, or do external forces have influence?

4. Why would you not make a deal with the devil?

A Message of Hope

IT IS EASY to give up hope. We read about corruption and feel cheated. We read about hate and violence, and feel anger and fear. We wonder how the world will get better, and count our blessings for just being safe. According to most of the news, the world is a pretty bad place to be.

It is easy to give up hope, but we must not. The power of thought is greater than you can imagine. Thoughts of hope can cut through the haze of fear and anguish. Hope has carried humankind through the darkest of days and hope will prevail now. Our desire for survival overcomes our fears about tomorrow and we persist.

You are not alone in your search for hope. Our mass consciousness has been in shock for years and the strain is showing. Security is tighter everywhere and we have conformed to rules. Every day, we read about people dying before their time, their lives taken for some cause or reason. The death of masses shocks us to the core, but it is the death of individuals that has the most impact.

I find solace in the knowledge that light feels better than dark. I have loved and I have hated and love feels better. I have both scorned and supported and supporting feels better. Courage feels better than fear, healing feels better than harming and happiness feels better than sorrow. Most people have experienced a range of emotions and know which ones feel better. In our actions, there is a knowing that goes deeper than conscience.

The most important aspect of retaining hope is the ability to return to the moment. Realize that all thoughts about past and future are simply brain waves and shut them down for the moment. Adjust your posture, take a deep breath, and balance your energy. Begin to understand the workings of your mind.

From your quiet moment of peace, all thoughts are initiated. Both hope and despair are constructs of your mind, created by the thoughts that are given priority. Any evaluation is judgment and the good or bad of any situation can be debated. All that really matters is your choice to create feelings of hope or feelings of despair.

I choose hope. It feels better.

Transformation Exercises

1. Move into meditative state and stop all mind chatter for one full minute.

2. Once the mind is quieted, maintain awareness of your thoughts. If required, shift your thoughts in a direction that feels good.

3. Maintain thoughts of hope and joy for ten minutes.

The New Spirituality

OUR SPECIES IS progressing at a rapid pace. All around the world people are awakening to a new spirituality. It is spirituality based not on religious faith but on compassionate feeling, spirituality based on remembering and understanding who we are. We begin to realize that we are not alone and separate, but are instead connected to everyone and everything in our world.

The old regimes of politics and religion, which are based on power and control, will resist the change. The way that things are now results from outdated belief systems that allow rule through fear. Contrasts are great between the world that we desire and the world that we observe. However, as our spiritual awareness grows, we will become even more conscious of disparity, until a critical mass is reached and the world awakens as one.

While everyone must have the right to grow and progress spiritually, complete individual freedom is not paramount. Free will is limited as there will be rules to follow. However, it is important that rules are used not to control individuals but instead to encourage positive growth for all. For a society to be peaceful and just, there must be a sense of order. For people to lead a safe and happy life, they must be protected from intimidation and abuse.

The paradox is that once everyone has reached a spiritual plateau, there will no longer be the desire to intimidate or abuse. Once people have remembered creative abundance, there will be no need to steal. Once people have recognized oneness, there will be no desire to harm another. Though the days may look dark, we are on a path of spiritual awakening that cannot be stopped.

Transformation Exercises

1. Describe your spiritual path.

2. Make a list of five people whom you consider to be spiritual.

3. What qualities do all five have in common?

4. How is their spiritual path similar to and different from yours?

Spiritual Guidelines

UNLIKE MOST RELIGIONS, spirituality is open to the interpretation of individuals. What feels right for one may not feel right for another, yet neither way is superior. The uniqueness of individuals is one of our blessed gifts. It is important that people be allowed to follow their chosen path.

However, though each person may choose to celebrate spirituality and existence in their own way, there are certain guidelines that a spiritual person will follow. These common elements of spirituality are what allow each person to be both unique, yet still a positive contributor to the common good.

Human rights are paramount. Once the masses realize that we are all connected, spiritually and energetically, we will realize that harming one harms us all. As people become spiritual, violence will diminish.

Spirituality is not religion. It is not faith in a particular book, its interpretations, or a set of rules. Instead, spirituality is a way of being that can be absorbed into all world religions. As a result, spirituality enhances rather than replaces all religions.

There is more than one way. Spirituality celebrates the uniqueness of the individual. It does not matter if you are Christian or Muslim, Democrat or Republican, short or tall,

black or white. Regardless of what defines you as a person, there is a spiritual path open to you.

Do not judge others. Their way is okay too. As long as someone does not harm another, their personal choices are their own business. Religious beliefs, sexual orientation, career, lifestyle, diet and other aspects of self are each person's own business.

Ultimately, spirituality is love. When your thoughts, words, actions and beliefs all resonate with love, you are becoming spiritual. When your love is complete with no exceptions, you have experienced spiritual progress. When you exist in love with everything at all times, you have reached a spiritual plateau.

Transformation Exercises

1. What makes you a spiritual person?

2. What are the most important aspects of spirituality?

3. Talk about a person who is very different from you and identify their spiritual elements.

An Elephant Tied

MANY YEARS AGO, people got excited when the circus came to town. Usually traveling overnight between towns, the circus would arrive and lay claim to a field, somewhere beyond the town limits. They would make camp close enough to draw townspeople, but distant enough to avoid municipal rules. A trip to the circus was an event, a change in realities that required some walking.

The circus would arrive with confined animals such as lions and tigers. The felines would roar as they padded around their cage, and let any observer know that attack was imminent if only the cage door were open. There were other animals that walked freely, or were kept in place with minimal effort. One of these animals was the elephant.

There it would stand, towering above all others, eating from a bale of hay. One could easily see the chain that led from the elephant's ankle, attached to a wooden stake. Though large and mighty, the animal stayed tethered, victim of an illusion.

When the elephant was young, the trainers had attached a rope to its hind leg. The rope was then tied to a stake in the ground. The baby elephant was placed just a little too far from its mother, and a little too far from the food. It would pull at the rope, over and over again, trying to escape from its shackles. But the rope was too strong, and the wooden peg had been hammered deep into the ground.

So the young elephant learned patience. Once he knew that escape was impossible, he gave up trying. Sometimes he would make sounds, trying to get the trainers attention. Sometimes this would work, and the trainer would feed him. But if the master was away, the elephant would stand patiently, only trying to reach things that were close.

What the elephant failed to realize was that the rules had changed. The rope that could hold a small baby elephant would have snapped with the slightest attempt, if only the grown-up elephant had tried. The peg that had held so tightly against juvenile tugs would crack easily under any strain from the adult. But he knew that escape was impossible, and that any attempts were futile and frustrating. So he stayed, locked into place by an illusion, waiting for handouts.

Transformation Exercises

1. Choose a specific past experience that has you tethered.

2. What do you believe makes this memory a challenge?

3. How do your beliefs limit your progress?

4. Which of your beliefs may be an illusion?

Creation

'As we move toward our dreams, we move towards our divinity.'

Julia Cameron, 'The Artist's Way', 1992.

The Clouds

ONE DAY, A man was sitting in a field, looking at the clouds and dreaming about a better life. He gazed at the sky and watched the fluffy white shapes changing as they moved, twisting and overlapping as they drifted through the sky. He saw many shapes in the clouds, and started to play a game. The first shape looked like a horse, and the one next to it resembled a chariot. If there were reins running between the two clouds, it would truly look like a horse and chariot.

Just as he was thinking about how the shapes could be improved, a breeze gusted and four thin lines began to extend from one of the clouds. In amazement, the man sat up and recognized that the clouds had formed to match his vision. It seemed impossible, but he had changed the clouds just by thinking about them.

The man started to experiment, and the clouds above began to move in strange patterns. A cloud that looked like a fish grew sails and turned into a yacht. Another cloud that looked like a mouse began to scurry across the sky, and the dark round cloud nearby suddenly grew paws and claws, grabbing the mouse-cloud and absorbing it.

Before he knew it, the man had spent the entire afternoon playing with the clouds, and realized that it was time to get home. He had many chores and responsibilities, and as he thought about his duties, he began to feel sad. He wished that he had control over his life, and that everything was just a little bit easier. As he walked across the field towards his house, the clouds settled into silence, wondering why their friend had given away his power.

Transformation Exercises

1. How does the story of the Clouds apply to your life?

2. What powers do you have that are not fully utilized?

3. Levitate this book.

You Can Change Your World

MOST PEOPLE EXPERIENCE pain, fear, guilt and anger. Much of these feelings exist due to misconceptions. When people achieve a greater understanding of these misconceptions, these feelings can diminish and go away. While heavy emotions can help us identify areas that require focus, it is not necessary to activate these emotions at all times.

All people are the center of their universe. While we realize that we are only one person and see the world around us, we still apply everything to ourselves. It is necessary to be self-centered to survive. Humans have been thinking about themselves since the beginning of time.

Whatever we see, hear, feel, touch and smell enters our awareness through filters. The first filter of choice decides where we focus our attention. There are many sources of input in our environment and we only allow some of them to consciously influence us. Once we have chosen input, we begin to evaluate and categorize.

Within our minds are many thoughts. As these thoughts begin to move in patterns, we experience feelings. Current feelings are matched with past memories and amplified. Different thoughts create different feelings and we store memories to use as tools for creating emotions. We perceive the world from our own perspective, formulating stories that support our belief systems.

As we create our world, there are many influences. Every experience you have had in your life is stored in your mind, shaping how you look at each situation. Everything you have been taught is with you, whether you believe it or not. Psychological tests have proven that people will alter their behavior based on false information, even when the falsehood is revealed. Doubts can be created in your mind even if the facts presented were untrue or later recanted.

Much of our belief system is based on our ego. We believe that the world revolves around us. We believe that we have influence where we do not, and we believe that everyone else's issues and concerns include us. They do not. Not everything is about us.

When you sit in silence and watch the world, energy is constantly moving. People are always interacting, weather is always changing, trees are always growing. In silence we can sit in peace and realize that none of our issues and concerns really matter to the world. The world goes on with or without us.

From that moment of peace and silence it is you who decides what to add to the world. You choose to attach to the moving energy; you choose to carry the flavor of the moment. Which thoughts do you emphasize? What input do you choose to focus on? What feelings do you choose to generate?

Within our cellular memories are events and experiences that have shaped who we are. We can recall stories with extreme detail as we relive moments from our past. Within these moments are emotions that we have carried for years. There comes a time when it is no longer necessary to carry this energy. It can be released simply by allowing it to go away.

The world is large and no one individual can change it all. What you can change is your experience. How the world treats you is directly related to how you treat the world. Enter it with enthusiasm, confidence and compassion and you will receive back your greatest desires. You CAN change your world and the world will change with you.

Transformational Exercises

1. Make a list of your bad qualities. What do you not like about yourself?

2. Make a list of your good qualities. What do you like about yourself?

3. Compare the lists, determining which statements are true and which have been given to you or reinforced by other people.

How We Create Our Life

WHILE EVERY DAY is different, sometimes there are milestone events that signify dramatic change. Occasionally, these events seem random, and we question why things happen. A traumatic experience or unexpected good fortune may come our way and we wonder 'what we have done to deserve such feelings?'

What we often fail to notice is how many of the occurrences in our life have been contrived. We sometimes create a sequence of events leading towards change. When the change occurs, our life may or may not improve. Either way, our path and learning experiences are different. What we need to understand is that often we have caused the change to happen.

A few years ago, I was working at a job and was stressed out. My mood had shifted from satisfaction and joy to confusion and anger. I began to be bothered by little things. I was frustrated with management and customers and co-workers. I was unhappy, which helped me find even more things to complain about. I regularly suffered headaches and my friends noticed a difference in my attitude.

Then, a wise man said to me 'You are looking for ways to be angry about this job'. He was right. For the previous few years, the job had been satisfying. Then I realized that the job had not changed, I had. I no longer desired my current path and allowed dissatisfaction to create anger. Once I started looking, there were lots of things to complain about and lots of people to blame.

Sometimes we get so angry that we quit our job, or try to find a new one. Other times our anger may influence other people, leading to being fired or laid off. Whatever events come to pass, it is necessary to realize that the change was driven by personal focus. By choosing our perception, we direct our feelings.

Making extreme lifestyle changes is not easy. Sometimes we are afraid to make the choices that we want to make. By focusing your energy on the things that will cause the change to happen, you build emotions that are strong enough to shift your path.

It is possible that we are correct in our perceptions. There is very little that can't be rationalized from one viewpoint or another. Individual perceptions may conflict, but most situations have more than one side. Misunderstandings are always a result of differences in perception. What one person sees as irrelevant, another sees as critical. What one sees as normal may be offensive to another.

The key to understanding how we create our life is recognition and awareness. Try to determine if you are creating emotions in order to achieve a change. If you find yourself focused in anger or feeling animosity, choose to look objectively at the situation. What are your personal triggers that let this anger surface? What needs are being filled and what direction do these emotions lead you? While another person may be doing something irritating, there is always something within that allows the irritation to affect you.

Anger is a great motivator and can be very productive. I once started a company from the ashes of another, primarily because of my personal anger about the situation. In retrospect, all of my anger was self-created. The issues that I chose to focus on were of my own making. There were other people involved, but it was how I chose to perceive their actions that affected the outcome.

When the wise man advised me that I was creating unhappiness, I examined my anger and found a solution. I wanted to change my path. Instead of creating animosity that would lead to my departure, I simply decided to resign. If you discover that your anger is leading you towards change, it is often simpler to just make the change.

Anger is not the only emotion that we can create. Think of the actions you have taken to move yourself towards joy or love or satisfaction or ecstasy. By choosing where to focus your attention, you direct the emotions that you feel and create the life that you desire.

Transformation Exercises

1. Are you happy with your job?

2. What would make you happier?

3. If you carry anger with you, where is that anger leading you?

4. Is there an easier way to deal with the situation?

The Bright Side of Life

WE ARE HERE because we are alive. It seems like such a simple statement and yet it is true. I think, therefore I am. You exist as a being of matter, a physical presence that can influence its external world. Your reason for being alive is simply to be, to exist and to experience. Nothing will be judged. Nothing really matters. We are all here just for the experience.

We try so hard to find purpose in our life. We think and we read and we pray. We cast horoscopes and visit psychics and talk to friends. We try to figure out the answer. We ask the question 'What should I be doing?' Ultimately, we discover that there is no answer. At least, there is no answer that someone else can give us. We must find our answers within ourselves. As for discovering the purpose of your life, it is less of a 'finding' and more of a 'choosing'.

The path that you choose is yours. Every day there are countless options to take. Every day there is an opportunity to change the direction of your life. Is this choice pre-determined, something that is fated to be? I think not. What occurs next is up to you.

We all have milestone days in our lives, days that we remember as turning points. If you look back and evaluate, you often find that a milestone event was the result of a series of previous activities. Getting a new job, getting married, having a child, graduating from school, or other such accomplishments are rarely instantaneous events. Each had a buildup and many options were available to you. Getting to the milestone event involved a series of decisions, choices and actions.

There are other milestones that we look back on a little less favorably, such as getting fired from a job, breaking up with a girlfriend or spouse, failing a course at school, or 'sudden' illness. In retrospect, we see that unfavorable milestones are also the result of a series of thoughts, actions, and choices. Just like the favorable milestones, the unfavorable outcomes were often arranged. Of course, sometimes things happen to us that appear to be out of our control. In these situations, the only responsibility we have is to incorporate the changes into our lives.

Life has meaning when you give it meaning·

This is all that really matters. Everything you do is a choice. How you evaluate your actions is a choice. Feeling good or bad about aspects of your life is a choice. Focusing your efforts in one direction or another is a choice. You know who you want to be, you know what types of things you want to do (or at least you know the things that you don't want to do). Follow your feelings and aim at feeling good about yourself and your actions.

Choices that you make directly influence your life. Ultimately, you are responsible for the results of these choices. If you choose to drop out of school, you must accept the path that unfolds. Even though there may be others involved who directly influence the outcome, you decided to allow the influence.

What is the magic in these statements? Your life is yours to create. You can identify the steps to take and then take them. The driving force in your life is your belief system. You do what you think is the right thing to do, at all times. You may take risks, and later rethink the action, but at the time you were certain. Change your belief system and you change your life.

The things that matter to you in life are a choice. Some people love their family, while others do not. Some people have lots of friends, while others do not. Some people have pets, and some do not. Some people make more money than they need, and others do not. Everything you have in your life is unique to you. There are others who may experience similar things, but the difference in every interaction is you.

Recognize your uniqueness, and let it shine.

Transformation Exercises

1. Describe where you are in your life at this moment.

2. What additional experiences do you wish to accumulate?

3. What issues are influencing your life today?

4. What outcomes are being set up by your current involvements?

Say What You Mean

How WE SHAPE our thoughts has a direct influence on the life that we experience. On a regular basis we do what is called thinking. In our mind we are analyzing, comparing, remembering, or deciding. What often goes unrecognized is the degree of judgment, expectation and perception that affects the process. As we verbalize our thoughts, inherent beliefs reveal their influence. We may intend our words to have one meaning, but the way that we say it has another.

On one occasion, I told a joke to a friend. 'What does the snail say when it is on the turtle's back? The answer that I gave was 'Wheee!' A few days later, I heard a friend repeat the joke, only his punchline was 'Whoa!' Can you hear the difference? A slight change in vowels alters the intent of the joke and reveals the feelings of the speaker. How we express words affects how we experience life.

If we examine our past, and tell people that it was horrible, we retain that energy. Now there is one more person who knows we suffer. If we meet new people and immediately give long-winded details of our problems, we are choosing to keep these memories active. Instead of changing our mode of thinking, we are drawing other people into our melodrama.

I once listened to a friend addressing a group of strangers. A year earlier she had taken stress-leave from work and was nearing recovery. Within minutes of speaking to the group, she apologized about something irrelevant and then revealed her illness as an excuse for her mistake. What I found interesting is that no one in the group knew the speaker, much less her medical history. Had the speaker not mentioned her past experiences, the group would have perceived her differently.

Are you aware of the limitations in your speaking habits? As we speak, there is a tendency to phrase things in certain ways, to repeat our beliefs, and to define our position. I need a job. I have no money. I am broke. I wish things were better. If only I were happier. Why can't

81

things work out? If only I could catch a break. Why do these things happen to me?

Each of the statements has implied perceptions and limitations. When we say things in a certain way, the words influence the outcome. If we believe the limitations in our phrasing, our actions reflect our beliefs, and we prove ourselves correct. If you feel that no one will hire you, you are right. If you feel that you have a lot to offer, you are right as well. If you think you can or think you can't, you are right.

Many words in our language have implied limitations. Words such as 'need' or 'problem' or 'detest' or 'advice' have implications that reveal our true beliefs. For example, 'advice' often implies the judgment that 'my way is better than yours'. Start to become aware of how you say things and how you limit yourself. Identify your belief system and how it influences your speech. Change the true intention of your words and say what you really mean.

The first step towards positive creation is to become aware of how you verbalize thoughts. Listen to what you say and how you say it. Listen again to what others say, and how there are implications woven into the words and tone. Statements can be posed as questions, implying an expected answer. 'You wouldn't want to help me, would you?'

The intention of your words is often based on inner belief, which has been developed through past experience. Previous rewards and punishments are remembered, even if the connection was only superstitious or coincidental. We learn that certain behaviors can have expected results. Our beliefs become part of us, and influence all of our perceptions and decisions.

In many cases, our beliefs are not based on actual experience. Opinions are accepted as truths, and other people's beliefs are passed on. Issues of self-esteem, fear, anxiety, and passionate conviction are often based on verbal interactions. By identifying and examining our beliefs, we may decide to change them.

By raising awareness, you can recognize your patterns. When you see that you have attached limitation to your thoughts, realize that the reality you manifest will follow your subconscious intention, even if it is different from what you consciously desire. By changing a phrase, you can effectively redirect energy.

Transformation Exercises

1. Make a list of stories you have told over the past few days, identifying the topic of the story and who you were telling the story to.

2. What feeling were you trying to evoke from the listener?

3. What feeling were you expressing as you told the story?

4. What energies do you think you created?

Make It So

I WOULD LIKE a new car. Though I am not really unhappy with my current car, mechanical costs have become frequent and the paint is starting to peel. The tires are slightly bald, and one slowly deflates. Every week or so I am at the gas station, kneeling beside the air dispenser.

What if I want to change this aspect of my life? What if I simply decide to refocus and bring a shiny new car into my life?

The process of manifestation is a cycle. Thoughts become words become actions become manifest. It really is quite simple. Though there are distractions and resistance along the way, we are in control. How many times have we changed our mind, or talked ourselves out of doing something? Have you had an idea and done nothing, only to see someone else create your vision? The frustration that we feel seeing others succeed is often the realization that we could be there as well.

When we don't get what we desire, the manifestation cycle is incomplete. We can choose to halt manifestation at any level. If we fail to persist, it is because we decide not to continue. Though barriers can appear, one who is truly focused gets around them. Think of any great accomplishment by a human and recognize the intent and energy required to succeed. Even things that look easy could require more steps than you know.

Our thoughts can become negative and potential ideas discarded. Our social training teaches us to look from a certain viewpoint. Biases are difficult to overcome. Once we deem a task unachievable or unworthy of our efforts, we have discarded manifestation.

At the word level, we can phrase things in a limiting manner. Saying that you 'need' something implies that you are dependent on it. Saying that you 'want' something still implies attachment to the outcome. Saying that you 'would like' something instead means that you will be fine with or without it. While I would like a new car, I am not really attached to the outcome. When I need a new car, I become more desperate and act accordingly.

Many people inhibit manifestation through inaction. Whether it is from guilt, doubt, other interests, or simply not knowing how, when we fail to act on a desire, we give it up. Everything that you have in your life is there because you went and got it. Of course there are presents and surprises, but the relationship that led to the presents required focus as well. If you want something to manifest, you must take action. Simply desiring or wishing isn't enough.

At all points in the cycle, you will rationalize why you should quit. I don't have enough money. I can't afford it right now. My car is just fine. Perhaps I should look for a used car. Lets wait for a while. Each time I rationalize a reason not to get a new car, I make the choice of whether or not to continue.

Now that I have begun the thought pattern, thoughts manifest into words. What type of car do I want? What color and style? Where can I get this car? What would the payments be? As I begin to think of the questions to be answered, the actions are easily defined.

Money is not even a consideration. It is not that I expect a car to magically appear in my driveway full of champagne and balloons. Rather, I have identified the steps that I can take without investment. Instead of letting the barriers stop me before I have started, I can simply begin the process of shopping. The barrier of money will be dealt with when it becomes an issue.

Once again, the process of manifestation is thought-words-action-manifestation. Stray from the path or decide to quit, and you eliminate the goal. It is okay to change your mind, but realize that the choice to persist or not is ultimately yours.

I don't intend to imply that there is any magic involved in the creation of your life. It is simply a matter of choice. When you see me pull up in a shiny new car, you will know if I chose blue, red or gray.

Transformation Exercises

1. Make a list of all the material things you would like to have. Be imaginative and abundant. Make the list as long as possible, ignoring cost or value discussions.

2. Categorize each item as A, B, or C, with 'A' meaning 'I really require this in my life to feel complete', 'B' meaning 'I would like this thing, but I can live without it', and 'C' meaning 'I don't expect to ever own this item in my life'.

3. Evaluate the size of each category and the feelings they evoke.

4. Do the emotions and desires stimulate creation?

5. Evaluate your feelings about possessions.

6. Pick one thing to manifest, then do so.

Note:

Shortly after writing this article, my car broke down for the last time. As it was being towed from my driveway to a place called 'Car Heaven', my father expressed regret for my situation. I replied that I was just making room in my driveway for a new car and he looked at me like I was crazy. At the time I was broke and unemployed, and buying a car was totally out of the question.

Three months later, I pulled into my driveway in a new car. I had signed a business contract that guaranteed income for two years. I used the contract as collateral to sign a car lease, and with no money down drove away in my new car. It really was quite simple.

Take It To The Limit

THERE ARE MANY ways that you can choose to lead your life. You can lead a conservative methodical life, slowly but surely working towards your goals. You can lead an erratic life, jumping from one thing to the next without really completing anything. You can be adventurous or cautious, industrious or lazy. You can take many risks, or no risks at all.

There is no right or wrong in your decision. It is not up to me or anyone else to determine how you should lead your life. While your choices have a direct impact on your experiences, only you know what you want. What you choose to accomplish is up to you and it is only you that must be content. There will always be people who tell you that you are not doing enough, or that you are doing the wrong thing. Though it is pertinent to listen to the advice of others, it is really your own happiness that matters.

There are many factors that influence the choices we make. Our training through youth and early adulthood defines what is good or productive or moral. What is progressive in some cultures is regressive in others. Friends and family offer their opinions and will surely tell you if you are out of line. The media regularly implies which lifestyles are right and wrong. The culture in which you were raised helps shape your life and your view of what you should do.

This is not to say that all external influences are wrong. Some advice is good and can have a positive influence if followed. Getting a good education is one cultural expectation that I personally have found valuable. However, the definition of a good education varies. To some, higher education in liberal arts or practical science defines the worth of a person. To others, specialization in a trade leads to admiration and security.

Ultimately, the answer comes down to you. What do you want from your life? What brings you satisfaction? Is your happiness based on the size of your house and bank account, or is it based on the number of people that you help and influence? If you feel happy with your progress and your path, you are doing fine. If not, only you can make the appropriate changes. While you may have assumed responsibilities that guide your lifestyle, remember that those responsibilities were also your choice.

Is your self-worth measured numerically, in comparison to the accomplishments of others? There will always be someone with more and someone with less. Lots of people had more money than Mother Theresa. Most people have more freedom than Michael Jackson. Many people have more close friends than Bill Gates. We cannot judge the accomplishments of others based on our own parameters, nor should others judge our choices.

There are two things that hold us back from achieving our goals: self-esteem and fear. Sometimes, we do not get what we want because we are afraid of failure. Other times, it is not fear that holds us back, but feelings of unworthiness. We doubt our capabilities, and fail to even take the first step. Unfortunately, letting fear or doubt control our path ensures that our dreams will not come true.

Once we decide what we want, and convince ourselves that we are worthy of our dreams, we can make the choice to move forward. Every goal is possible if the proper steps are taken. True, there are some goals that are unrealistic. It would be difficult for me to be the youngest person to run across the country. But if running across the country were a desire, I am sure I could do it. Others with less physical prowess have accomplished more.

When you identify your desires, the only limits that exist are the ones that you accept or impose upon yourself. Take your life to the furthest limit. Dream big dreams and work towards them. When you reach the end of your life, don't let your desires be unfulfilled because you didn't try. The only true failure in life is not taking the first step. Choose what you want, and move towards it.

Transformation Exercises

1. What do you want to achieve in your life?

2. In your list of desires, which ones existed a year ago? (Two years, Five Years...)

3. What prevents you from achieving your goals?

4. What choices can you make to guide your self towards your desires?

Bessie and the Carrot

BESSIE WAS A mule, and very proud of it. Her mother was a beautiful white mare, the proudest and fastest horse in the group. Her father was a donkey, strong and proud and patient. They were both special animals on the farm, and Bessie had the best of both of them.

From her father, she inherited the stamina and toughness of a donkey. She also got his ears. From her mother, she inherited the eloquence and grace and speed of the horse. Together, Bessie was both fast and strong, the most versatile equine on the farm.

Every day, a young boy would saddle her up and climb on her back. He would tie a string around a carrot, and then tie the other end of the string to a long stick. Bessie was excited. Food was right in front of her eyes. All she had to do was move towards it.

Bessie was strong, and could walk for miles and miles. Around her, the green of the forests flashed by as she focused on the carrot. It hung in front of her and was almost achievable. At some point, after a considerable walk, the boy would get off of her back and give her the carrot. Bessie wasn't quite sure what caused the boy to stop, because it was different almost every time. All Bessie knew was that if she kept walking, she would eventually get the carrot.

One day, the boy made a mistake. He went into a building and forgot to watch his mule. He also forgot to put away the carrot and the stick. The carrot was swinging in the wind directly in front of Bessie's eyes. She had to have it.

She started to step slowly towards the carrot, and as it moved, her pace increased. She went from walk to trot to full gallop in mere moments, reaching for her goal. She felt lighter without the boy on her back. This time she knew she would catch the carrot.

The race continued on for some time and Bessie became lost. She finally did get the carrot, when the string snagged in a branch and the carrot stopped moving. Now she was alone in the woods, ready for her next step.

Which way should she go? The carrot was gone, and there was nothing to walk towards anymore. Before she could move, she had to decide which way to go. She was used to standing in one place, when the boy would tie her to a post and leave. She was very comfortable sleeping on her feet and the warm sunshine made it very pleasant.

As Bessie decided which way to go, she began to look around, searching for a target. She saw some grass that looked rather tasty and those small leaves on the bush feel really good on the gums. Everywhere she looked there was a carrot, or a haystack, or a bush. She moved in all directions, tasting this and tasting that. She moved in circles through the forest, looking and seeing for the first time. Bessie didn't know what to do. There were too many things to choose from, and she couldn't make up her mind. So she went to sleep.

When she woke, the boy was stroking her mane and talking to her gently. He climbed onto her back and the familiar carrot suddenly appeared in front of her face. She was ecstatic. Bessie felt comfortable and warm and secure. She knew what to do.

Bessie walked off, along the trail and out of the forest. The weight of the boy on her back felt comfortable and the carrot looked delicious. Sometimes, it is easier when you are focused on one carrot.

There are limitless goals to select from and it is up to you to choose your direction. Some may take the comfortable and secure route, while others taste everything. Sometimes those who are on the secure route forget that there are other options. And sometimes people like me need to be reminded that it is okay to follow one carrot at a time.

Transformation Exercises

1. List three goals that are important to you now.

2. Rank them in importance.

3. Make a list of the steps required to achieve each goal.

4. Set a time frame for each goal.

5. Take the first step towards your most important goal.

Resolutions

THOUGH PEOPLE BRAVELY make resolutions for change on New Year's Eve, revisiting resolutions can reveal success or failure. Did you decide to lose weight, to exercise more, to quit smoking, or go to bed early? Perhaps you resolved to date more often, to argue less, to spend less money or to make more phone calls. Whatever your resolution, it is likely that within the first month you have disappointed yourself and given up for another year.

It is a standard tradition to make resolutions about the upcoming year. In many cases, the goals involve changes that we want to make, or activities that we want to eliminate. Year after year the same issues keep coming up and we finally decide that this is the year that everything will change. Unfortunately, you made the same promises to yourself last year.

I recently spoke with some people who have given up on resolutions. The general feeling was that there was no point making them, as the resolve to complete the goal wasn't really there. The arbitrary date of January 1st just wasn't strong enough to help each of these people bring about the changes desired, so they decided to accept the parts of themselves that they really wished were different.

This year, I felt that common resolutions and goals were not enough and was determined to find out why. Goal setting is not only about changing behavior; it is about deciding what to do with your time, effort and focus. I realized that most resolutions are about doing or not doing, while my state of mind is about being. The actions that we plan, or the actions that we deny, are ultimately a statement of who we are. The real question is 'Who do you want to be?'

I decided that I would focus more on my core being and let the activities and actions that result occur naturally. Our state of being is directly within our control. Though we may be influenced by external sources, we can always refocus our thoughts. How we feel is directly related to our perception and attitude. Whatever we experience, the resulting feelings are ours to choose. This year, rather than stating what I will do, or what I will not do, I instead choose to state what I will be.

I will be happy, as happiness is totally within my control. No matter what events or experiences come my way, I am glad to be alive.

I will be productive. Obviously, I will do further work defining the tasks that I will focus on, but no matter what I choose to do, I am in control of my efforts.

I will treat people with love, compassion and understanding. How I choose to perceive others, and how I react to them, is entirely within my control. By reducing or removing my expectations, I remain in control of my personal experiences. Of course there are things that influence me, but initially I choose to look at each person as a beautiful soul on a journey through life.

I will be spiritual and stay connected to my higher self. There are many things in our daily lives that seem to get in our way, to direct our thinking or our actions. None of them matter. By living in the moment and following my inner guidance, the pleasures of life come to the surface.

Of course, there are many specific goals that I have for the year. Some will come to fruition and others will not. By choosing where we direct our energy, we can manifest that which we want. If instead we focus on what we do not want, we are making the statement that we feel trapped. Focus on lacking and you will experience lacking. Focus on eliminating desires and they will rule you.

The discipline of removing activities from your life, whether it is smoking or overeating or some other bad habit, only serves to remind you that you still have a habit. Instead, by choosing to be healthy, those behaviors are more easily eliminated. This year, instead of deciding what you don't want, choose to determine what you do want and make it happen.

Transformation Exercises

1. Make a list of five characteristics that support who you want to be.

2. Make a list of five characteristics that do not support who you want to be.

3. Describe the effort that it takes to maintain the characteristics that you like about yourself.

4. Describe the barriers that keep the unwanted characteristics in your life.

5. List five characteristics that could replace the unwanted ones.

Being There

In the book 'Jonathan Livingston Seagull', the title character yearns to fly faster than any other gull in history. He keeps perfecting his technique and of course he keeps getting faster and faster. However, even when he reaches speeds inconceivable to other gulls, he is disappointed as he realizes that he still has limits. When he meets an older, wiser gull who demonstrates instantaneous transportation, he is told that 'perfect speed, my son, is being there'.

In our linear minds, travel requires transition and time and effort. While it is nice to think about being able to get from one place to another instantly, we know that it is physically impossible. Everything we have heard and experienced tells us that we must take steps to get anywhere. Though some people can move faster than others, everyone takes time to change location.

If it takes time to change location, what about other changes that we desire? We all have a tendency to seek that which we do not have and to dream about getting there. However, the more that we wish we were somewhere else, the more that we separate ourselves from that reality. As we analyze where we want to be, we also identify the steps it will take to get us there. Often, the steps seem unachievable and we remain where we are.

Desire for change is often specific, such as wanting more money, more freedom, a bigger house or a better relationship. However, what we are really looking for are the feelings that we associate with our goals. A desire for more money usually indicates a need to feel more secure; a desire for a better job is often a longing to feel less stressed, or more fulfilled, or less unhappy.

Instead of spending your life perceiving what is missing, it is much more effective to identify which aspects of your life already create the feelings that you target. Instead of waiting for things to happen that will make you happy, just be happy. Instead of waiting for things to happen that will make you feel secure, just feel secure. The simplest of answers is often the most difficult to achieve, since we have practiced the feeling of lacking all of our lives. However, it is important to remember that the quickest way to get from A to B is to just be.

Transformation Exercises

1. Identify one change that you would like to make about yourself.

2. Identify another person who demonstrates the quality that you desire.

3. How is that person different from you?

4. What alterations would you need to make to your lifestyle to emulate that person?

Focus Pocus

IN A UNIVERSE of infinite possibility, it is easy to shift focus constantly. Each second of existence there are stimuli and distractions that call for our attention. Even when one is in silence, there are many internal voices wanting to be heard. Around us energy is constantly shifting, and as we ride the waves of quantum reality, it takes specific effort to aid manifestation.

At the first level of manifestation, it is necessary to focus on your desired outcome. Following the path of creation, thoughts become words become actions become manifest. As the path continues, there will be many chances to cease your efforts or change your desires. However, if one continually moves in a direction, the destination is usually reached.

Organization helps with focus. Setting daily, weekly, monthly and yearly goals can aid in productivity. There are always many choices for where our efforts go, and in a linear reality we only do one thing at a time. Even a solid hour of focus put towards a specific goal helps the creation. If you keep coming back to a project, eventually it gets done. The setting of timeframes and deadlines is also of great assistance in assuring the completion of a project.

However, most elements of organization and manifestation are considered from a third-dimensional reality. While we may think we are taking steps towards a particular creation, we may actually be creating barriers to our success. We may be sabotaging our efforts, or broadcasting conflicting messages that confuse those intending to help us. It becomes necessary to really understand your current motivations and feelings and then to create the feeling of success.

A Focus Wheel is a tool used for the creation of positive vibration regarding a specific desired outcome. Using pen and paper draw a circle. In the center write a positive statement about desired outcome, such as 'I am financially abundant'. Then, around the circle write sentences describing positive elements that lead to the desired outcome, such as

'I am smart with money' and 'Many financial opportunities come my way'. As you write down each statement, be very aware of how you feel about the statement.

When you are capable of creating a focus wheel full of positive statements that you truly believe, you are vibrating in a manner that encourages the fulfillment of your desire. As your activities continue, notice activities that do not match the vibration of your focus wheel and make the appropriate changes. Some changes require elimination of elements from your life, while others require only minor adjustments.

Moving in your desired direction contains elements of visualization, focus, and maintaining vibration. How can you be abundant when you vibrate poverty? How can you be successful when you vibrate doubt? Learn how to be aware of what your vibration is creating in your current reality and then move towards your preference. The possibilities are endless and you have much influence.

Transformation Exercises

1. Create a simple focus wheel that describes the fulfillment of a desire.

2. Once you have completed the wheel, describe your change in vibration.

3. Compare your focus wheel with others and discuss.

4. Create a new focus wheel.

Meditation and Balance

'What lies behind us and what lies before us are tiny
matters, compared to what lies within us.'

Ralph Waldo Emerson

Slow Down, You Move Too Fast

THE OLYMPIC MOTTO 'Faster, Higher, Stronger' can be taken literally. At every International sports competition, records are set. Milestones that seemed impossible are regularly surpassed. Some give credit to training techniques, others suspect drug enhancement, while a few recognize the development of our species. To put things in perspective, Mark Spitz, who set seven Olympic records for swimming in 1972, would not have qualified for the 2000 Olympic team.

Business advances at the same pace. The stock markets constantly change and values go up or down. Companies try to exceed their sales forecasts each year and push for more the next year. Have you ever heard of a salesperson having their targets reduced? No matter how much is achieved, everyone expects the next year to be even better. When a business does not succeed gloriously, it may crash and burn.

Crowded cities get busier. People rush around, pushing and shoving. Everywhere there are lineups and crowds with anxious people trying to get things done quickly. Parents trot through the shopping mall, angry with their children for slowing them down. Drivers continuously switch lanes, looking for a quicker route. Employers and customers always want something done 'yesterday'. It is no wonder that heart attacks are common.

I visited a friend recently who had decided to walk for his health. We went out for a 'leisurely stroll'. After the first mile I had to stop. We had been moving at an incredible pace, faster and faster along the sidewalk, swinging our arms and not noticing how hard we were breathing. Finally, I stopped and asked my friend to stop as well. He found it difficult, but agreed.

Though I blamed my fitness, it was really my intention of calmness that brought me to a halt. I then demonstrated how to 'walk like a monk', a technique taught to me by a Buddhist monk named 'Bhante', which means 'Spiritual Friend'. Walking slowly and deliberately, each step taken is matched exactly with the breathing. Right foot forward, breath in through the nostrils. Left foot forward, breathe out through the nostrils. Matching your breathing to your walking requires you to move slowly. Instead of walking with the intention of getting somewhere, I was taught to simply enjoy the movement. As I slowed down, I began to see more of the world around me.

What I began to notice was how much of a rush everyone was in. Around me were honking cars, swearing drivers and angry pedestrians. Unlike children who run for the joy of running, most adults rush because they feel that they have to get somewhere. Instead of appreciating where they are, or the journey that they are on, most people begrudge time, as it gets in their way.

Learning to have patience can be difficult. Usually, our thoughts are related to events and activities that exist away from where we are at the moment. When you go for a walk, are you really focused on where you are and what you are doing, or are you thinking about past or future activities? When you drive, is your main concern about getting there?

My suggestion is to slow down and take a look around. There are few things so important that they must be done immediately. What are you rushing for? Become aware of your pace as you walk, of your anxiety as you drive, of your need to speed up. Change your intention and begin to appreciate the moment. When you stop to smell the roses, check out everything else around you as well.

Transformation Exercises

1. Arrange a time where you have no other responsibilities except to just be.

2. Practice 'walking like a monk' in a natural setting.

3. Sit in a busy area and observe people rushing.

4. Ask someone in a rush to slow down and see what happens.

Clear Your Mind

THE OTHER DAY, I was ridiculed by a ten-year-old girl. As she was looking through my house, she got to the room with a carpet and no furniture and wanted to know what it was for. When I told her it was my meditation room, she laughed. 'You don't really meditate, do you?' she asked. When I said yes, she laughed again, and asked me if I could float in the air.

There are many misconceptions about meditation. Sometimes seen as the practice of Buddhist monks and people who are 'a wee bit touched', meditation is something that all people can benefit from. It helps calm the mind, reduces stress, balances the physical body, and enhances our ability for self-control in any situation. Meditation can also be the path to profound thinking, problem resolution, and enlightenment.

In Buddhist philosophies, the style of meditation called 'zazen' means 'just sitting'. The easiest position for meditation is sitting, either on the floor or in a chair. Meditation can be done while lying down (though you may fall asleep) or while standing, walking, or doing a repetitive task. Tai Chi is often called the moving meditation and allows for rhythmic motion while clearing the mind.

One of the standard debates about meditation is what you should be thinking about. In some philosophies, meditation should always be 'about something'. Whether the thoughts are related to specific issues (such as personal relationships or activities) or generic concepts (such as love or peace), meditation with thought concentrates on finding an answer.

Other beliefs contend that meditation should actually be about nothing. In eastern philosophy, the concept of 'dhyan', most closely interpreted as 'no-mind', implies that one should shut down all thoughts when meditating. This is the style that I prefer. To vacate the mind of thoughts allows one to disconnect from our daily melodramas and to simply just be.

For most people, our minds are constantly chattering. We think about many things as we plan, analyze, list, categorize, worry, anticipate and remember. Sometimes at night my mind goes through dozens of scenarios before falling asleep. Some of the thoughts are about things to come, but most of the thoughts are reliving old dramas and events. As Robert Heinlen said, 'I lay in bed doing what I call thinking, but probably is not'.

Mind chatter is often the source of stress, anxiety and depression. When we are worried or angry about something, we have a tendency to think about it over and over and over, creating emotional turmoil. We superimpose our own feelings on other people's situations, or we relive our most anxious moments. Though we say that we would rather not be in that space, we must enjoy it because we keep going there.

Meditation is a means of eliminating mind chatter. The actual practice of meditation can begin with a ritual or tradition, preparing for relaxation. My ritual involves the lighting of candles. Once in a comfortable position, focus your awareness on breathing. Breathe slowly and deeply through your nostrils, and then hold your breath momentarily. Exhale slowly and deeply through your mouth, and then again hold your breath momentarily.

In the beginning, you may find it difficult to stop thinking. Rather than resisting, try to achieve a separate awareness, becoming an observer of your thoughts rather than a participant. If you can identify your thoughts without becoming emotionally involved, it is easier to maintain control. When you discover yourself thinking about anything but your breathing, simply decide to put those thoughts away for later. Unless you are physically in danger, there is nothing that cannot wait for five or ten minutes before being analyzed.

I have practiced meditation enough that I can change my mood with one breath. Recently, I was sitting in a stalled car in heavy traffic, and everyone was honking and screaming at me. I briefly closed my eyes, took a deep breath and relaxed. Once I was centered and balanced, I was much more capable of dealing with the situation. The ability to relax and stop the mind is a definite advantage.

Transformational Exercises

1. What are your experiences with meditation?
2. What are your beliefs about meditation?
3. Practice clearing your mind.

A New Sensation

THE HUMAN BODY is a field of energy. Like all energy, each body vibrates with a particular resonance. Our resonance changes with mood and we feel different in different situations. The way we feel when we are angry is quite different from the way we feel when we are calm. Whether the changes are major or minor, throughout our life we are constantly changing and altering our vibration.

Sometimes we alter our mood through conscious thought. By focusing awareness on specific elements of our life, we change our feelings. By choosing to participate in certain activities, we direct our experiences and the sensations they create. By interacting with certain people, we stimulate emotions that become more intense.

Our physical environment directly influences our resonance. Sound and music alter the way that we feel. The colors around you affect your vibration. The temperature, humidity, and lighting around you have a direct effect. Everything that you can sense, and some things that you can't, has a direct impact on how you feel at the moment.

It is possible for you to filter out certain stimuli and focus your attention elsewhere, but harsh stimuli still has an effect. When working in a machine shop with loud repetitive noises, music can help the mind disconnect, but the body still feels the impact of the sound. Though perception and focus can alter your feelings, the only way to truly change the influence of environment is to change your environment. It is easier to relax by a stream in a park than it is to relax in a noisy crowded mall.

It is possible to increase awareness of your personal vibration. 'Checking-in' involves stopping periodically throughout the day to become aware of your feelings. Quite often, we have moments of transition when we finish one task and have to decide what to do next. After hanging up the telephone, become aware of the transition point. Take the opportunity to become aware of your feelings. Notice where tension is held; which areas feel good and which do not; and where you feel imbalanced.

Controlled breathing is an effective technique to help you relax while doing the check-in. With your eyes closed, breathe in through your nostrils to the count of four, hold for two, breathe out for four, and hold for two. Continuing this pattern allows you to focus your attention on your breath and to stop thinking about anything else. Then shift your awareness to each part of your body, noting how it feels. You may change your posture or stretch, and you may move into a more balanced position.

Concentrate on balancing and grounding. Visualize roots growing from the base of your spine, extending into the ground. Compare your sides, left to right, front to back, top to bottom, and notice any variations. Relax and allow yourself to achieve balance.

Once you have consciously checked in enough times, you get used to analyzing how you feel and it becomes automatic. The analysis covers your emotions at the time, rate of breathing, posture, the sensations from each part of your body, and where you are focusing your thought. After taking a snapshot of your current state, determine how to adjust. Any adjustments should increase your comfort level. If it feels good, do it.

It is fun to experiment with awareness of feelings. Try checking in, then playing a piece of music, and then checking in again to discover any differences. You may feel that your energy level has increased or decreased, or that your awareness has shifted to a different part of your body.

The mood or tone of a written article has a direct influence on the reader. Read the column of a staunch political reporter, and see how the writing affects your mood (particularly if you disagree). Then read a column from the Lifestyles section, about gardening or cooking or sex. Notice how your feelings change, and understand how the input has changed you. Your energetic pattern has been affected by the reading of words.

A heightened awareness of feelings is remarkable. Allowing your feelings and intuitive thoughts to guide your life is sometimes scary, but very fulfilling. Understanding how the energy of the body works is a fascinating journey, and 'I am only an egg'.

Transformational Exercises

1. Practice 'checking in' with yourself and learn how to evaluate your personal vibration.

2. Experiment with different external stimuli, and see how your vibration can be influenced.

3. Become aware of how your thoughts also affect your personal vibration.

4. Sit quietly in a public place and observe the vibrations of others.

'I Am Only An Egg'

IN ROBERT HEINLEIN's 'Stranger in a Strange Land', the hero Michael states 'I am only an egg'. His intention was to indicate that he was still young and inexperienced. He compared his level of learning to that of an embryo, with many wondrous discoveries available to explore. Even though his thinking was advanced, he knew that just around the corner was something else that would open his eyes. By the shape of my aura, and with my intention of growth, 'I am only an egg'.

Let's talk a little more about energy. When I visualize the human energy field, I see an egg-shaped aura surrounding each person. The aura exists in layers and there are multiple levels to each person's energy field. It is possible to see these layers if your aura reading skills are distinct and to feel these layers if you are energy sensitive. With training, openness, and intent, I have learned to feel someone's energy field with my hands (front and back) and face and to distinctly feel the disruptions and layers in the field.

The egg-shaped field surrounding us is indicative of our health and existence. The role of an energy healer is to help an individual strengthen their field and perhaps smooth out or release energetic issues. All people subconsciously feed energy into their field and many healers have learned how to efficiently charge themselves. By visualizing a strong golden light radiating from your body, you are taking positive steps to heighten your vibration. Energy follows intention and any intent to strengthen your field is helpful.

Once you have learned how to energize your own field, it is possible to learn how to help others. Healing energy should only be offered. A healer does not enforce his will on the recipient. During the session a healer moves into a balanced comfortable condition that the recipient can choose to emulate. In addition, the healer may offer surplus energy channeled from the environment. Like a sponge soaking up water, an energy field should be allowed to take only that energy that is desired and helpful. It is not up to the healer to determine someone else's path or vibration.

In most cases the effects of energy healing are subtle. But to discuss the role of a healer we shall use an extreme. Terry Fox was a Canadian teenager who lost a leg to cancer, then ran halfway across the country raising money before succumbing. What if a healer had chosen to fix Terry Fox's leg? If that had happened, Terry would never have made the contribution that he achieved with a determined soul. His bravery and courage still exist as a role model for thousands with similar afflictions. It is not up to any healer to choose the path of another. We can only assist when asked.

When visualization becomes comfortable, it is possible to send healing energy to other people. By definition, distance healing involves healing someone that you are not touching, even if they are sitting across the room. To me, the real step in distance healing is to work on someone who you cannot see. By creating and energizing an egg-shaped ball of energy around someone, you can help strengthen and stabilize their field.

Transformation Exercises

1. Practice sending healing energy to someone touching only their aura.

2. Practice sending healing energy to someone sitting across the room.

3. Practice sending healing energy to someone in another location (with or without picture).

Picture Yourself

THE WAY THAT we lead our life has a direct impact on our physical appearance. If we exercise and eat well, we are toned and healthy. Happiness can shine from our face. If we smoke or drink excessively, our pallor fades. Stress reflects in our complexion.

I once saw a portrait that a friend painted of her father. It was extremely well done, and though I have never met the man, I know what he looks like. He is distinguished looking, with graying hair and a kind face. What is really unique about this portrait is revealed when you cover half of the face with a blank sheet of paper. A mirror would be even better. When only the left side of the portrait (being the right side of his face) is visible, the portrait is of a young man, glowing with life and intensity. When only the right half is observed (or mirrored into a full face), the portrait is of a man aged and tired, finished with life.

In Oscar Wilde's story 'The Picture of Dorian Gray', a man encounters a unique situation. His face no longer ages. Instead, his portrait evolves throughout his life, reflecting his experiences. While his face remains young and beautiful, his portrait reflects the cruel and immoral behavior in the life led by Dorian Gray.

Much like Dorian Gray's picture, our face reflects the story of our life. In our personal story, the tales of the left side and right side of our faces are different. Our faces are not symmetrical. Try it. Get a portrait of yourself and cover one side at a time. You will be amazed at the different faces that are revealed. The effect is even more remarkable if you work with a digital image on the computer. Sometimes when you put mirror image pictures beside each other, it looks like two different people.

If our face is unbalanced, what about the rest of our body? There is a type of scale used by chiropractors that weighs each side of your body separately. Due to posture or imbalance, you may carry more weight on one side of the body than the other. When a friend of mine tried this,

his right side weighed fifty pounds more than his left side. Recently, that same friend was skiing, and injured his knee. He spent the next few weeks on crutches. Can you guess which knee he hurt? No, it was not the side with the extra weight. It was the other side. His right side is dominant and strong. It was his weaker left side that was injured.

Theoretically, the left side of our body represents our feminine aspects, the tendency to be creative, to be intuitive, and to nurture. The right side represents our masculine aspects, the tendency to be aggressive, to be logical, and to take action. The characteristics that we display often can be related to the dominance of one side over the other. When one side dominates the other in beliefs or action, physical imbalances can occur.

Balance is equilibrium. It is the attainment of a state in which opposing energies are present in equal strength. All of the holistic therapies aim at achieving balance. On a physical level, therapies such as massage, herbal medicines and chiropractic adjustments attempt to balance the posture and the internal workings of the body. On an energy level, therapies such as Reiki, Acupuncture and Therapeutic Touch attempt to balance our energy flow. Movement practices such as Yoga and Tai Chi strive towards the achievement of balance, both in the body and in the mind. On a spiritual level, such practices as meditation and visualization help us to achieve calmness and inner peace.

The first step in achieving personal balance is awareness. Begin to take notice of your weight distribution as you walk and as you stand. Compare how each side of your body feels. Which way are you leaning? Which side feels stronger? Become more aware of your habits and how you tend to move.

Bringing your life into balance must be a conscious effort. Only you can make a difference.

Transformational Exercises

1. Stand with your eyes closed and evaluate the balance of your body. Adjust your posture as necessary until you feel balanced.

2. Stand in front of a mirror, and evaluate visually whether you appear balanced.

3. Take a long slow walk and observe whether your left or right side feels dominant.

4. Try to switch back and forth between dominant sides.

A Question of Balance

OUR LIVES ARE constantly changing. We experience extremes and yet seek to regain balance. We try to balance our social life, our family life, and our finances. We try to stay fit and healthy, to reduce stress, and to increase creativity. Many of us recognize that our lives are out of balance, but don't know what to do. What we often forget is that balance is our natural state, and can be easily achieved.

When I was six years old, I got a new bicycle. Actually, it wasn't new. A boy down the street named Jimmy got a new bike and my dad bought the old one from Jimmy's father. But to me it was new, and represented a milestone of growing up. I now had a bicycle.

That day, I sat on the bike and tried to ride. My feet easily reached the pedals, but because of the crossbar, I had to tilt to one side, with one foot on a pedal and only one on the ground. To get started, I would first have to push the bike upright, and then start pedaling forward. I tried a few times and was unable to do it.

Then my dad came to help. He put both hands on the bike and started to walk forward. Since this was an old bicycle without gears, the pedals moved in unison with the wheels, and my feet began to move with them. Dad began to walk, and then to trot, and then to run.

I was peddling away like mad, my eyes fixed straightforward as I leaned into the handlebars. Then Dad let go, and I was on my own. I peddled for a bit, but then I got nervous, and started to look around. I fell off the bike into a grassy ditch, but was not hurt. For the first time, I had ridden a bike. Before the end of the day, I was able to ride without assistance. I had discovered how to keep balance on a moving vehicle.

For the next few years, I rode my bike almost every day. However, when I turned sixteen I learned how to drive. Soon the bicycle was put away, and the car became my mode of transportation. It was difficult to take a girl out on a date with a bicycle.

When I was thirty-five years old, I bought a new bicycle. I hadn't ridden a bike since I had received my driver's license nineteen years earlier. After years of driving a car, I realized that I missed the freedom of hopping on a bike. I missed riding to wherever my legs could take me.

I brought my new bike home in the car and then hopped on. I felt a bit wobbly at first, but by the time I had ridden to the end of the street, I had regained my balance. Though it had been many years since I had ridden a bike, I knew almost immediately how to do it again.

Once you achieve balance, you will always know how to regain it. The memory of balance is enough to guide you. It is not something you struggle to achieve. Instead, it is something you relax into. Simply becoming aware of your current state helps allow balance into your life.

It was pleasant learning how to ride a bike again and to regain my confidence in riding.

Unfortunately, I only rode that bike once or twice before it was stolen. Even when you regain balance, things change.

Transformational Exercises

1. Stand on one foot.

2. Remember a time in your life where you learned about balance.

3. Visualize yourself doing a physical activity where balance is required.

4. Stand on one foot.

The Druid Egg

THE DRUID EGG is a tool that can be used to help you find inner peace and contentment.

Based on concepts taught within the ancient Druid culture, the Druid Egg provides an object for complete focus, providing a method for calming the mind, enhancing awareness, and eliminating distracting thoughts.

The Druid egg is an egg-shaped piece of rock, usually marble, onyx or granite. The same size as an egg, it is to be held in the hand and stared at. As you gaze at the egg, relax your body and breathe deeply and evenly. By concentrating on the colors, lines, textures and shades, you provide yourself something to think about besides all of the other things that are going on in your head.

Each time you find your concentration shifting from the egg to other thoughts, bring your focus back to the specific details of the egg, and remain focused until all distractions fade away. As you learn to use this tool well, you will easily be able to turn off any mind chatter that affects your concentration.

The Druids determined that the best way to stay balanced and whole was to remain in a state of stillness and centeredness. Most thoughts are about yesterday and tomorrow, and thoughts tend to spiral and escalate, overcoming the reality of now and replacing it with manufactured thoughts that are often based on fear and doubt. If we only thought positive thoughts, and always felt optimistic and excited, then the Druid egg would not be necessary. However, since many people tend to move towards thoughts of disharmony, it becomes necessary to develop a way to stop the mind.

Your personal magic can be amplified as you learn how to stay in the present. Once you understand how to observe your environment without judgment, you begin to perceive the magic of the world and how you can influence it. Often seen by the uninitiated as simply a good luck talisman, the Druid Egg can become a tool for enhancing yourself, your life, and your world.

Transformational Exercises

1. Find a druid egg, or something similar.

2. Practice focusing concentration on the patterns of the object.

3. Take your egg into a public place and practice meditating there.

Perceptions

Boy: Do not try and bend the spoon. That's impossible.
Instead... only try to realize the truth.
Neo: What truth?
Boy: There is no spoon.
Neo: There is no spoon?
Boy: Then you'll see, that it is not the spoon that bends, it is only yourself.

The Matrix, 1999.

Rain Child

ARLEY WAS A little boy who did not like rain. It was cold and wet and stung his face. It left big puddles that soaked his feet. It prevented him from going outside to play. Every morning when he woke up, Arley would say to himself 'I hope it doesn't rain, I hope it doesn't rain'. Of course, sometimes when he opened his eyes, it was raining outside and Arley wondered why he was being punished this way.

One sunny day, Arley met a little girl named Aida. She was skipping and laughing as she danced through the field with a flower in her hand. She saw Arley standing under a tree, and called out to him 'Aren't you going to come out and play? It is such a beautiful day.'

Arley pointed at a cloud way off on the horizon. 'I would like to play, but I can't because it might rain'. Aida smiled and kept on playing.

The next day it actually was raining, and Arley was sad. Despite all of his wishing, the rain had come anyway, and Arley knew that the gods did not listen to his prayers. He looked out his window at the horrible weather. To his dismay he saw Aida dancing in the field. He wondered if she was crazy, then realized that perhaps she needed his help. He got dressed, donning boots and a sweater and a coat and a hat, and ventured out onto the field to rescue Aida.

When he got there, before he had a chance to say anything, Aida spoke to him. 'I am so glad that you came out to play. It is such a beautiful day.' Arley was confused, and told her so. 'It is not beautiful, it is a horrible day', he said with conviction. Aida just laughed, and raised her arms as she danced in a circle. 'Don't you know that the rain brings the flowers? Don't you realize that rain is god's gift of life?'

Arley shook his head and walked away. He went back inside, away from the rain and away from the strange little girl with the mixed up priorities. He knew that he was right, and that once again the rain was going to ruin his day. He looked out the window one more time, and muttered to himself, 'I sure hope that it doesn't rain tomorrow'.

Transformation Exercises

1. Is your behavior in the past week more like Arley or Aida?.

2. What lessons can we learn from Arley?

3. What lessons can we learn from Aida?

4. Choose an environment that you don't like, then give three reasons why someone else may like it.

Follow the Leader

WHAT IF YOU could look down at your life from above? Unencumbered by the context of your environment, you could see your life from a different perspective. What observations would you make about your path and potential?

While walking through the woods, I came upon a nest of tent caterpillars that had just opened. Dozens of tiny creatures, each about a quarter inch in length, swarmed over the silken pouch. They wandered aimlessly, bumping into and crawling over each other.

Finally, one of the caterpillars began to climb a branch. Almost immediately, another caterpillar followed. Soon there was a long line of caterpillars climbing up. As the leader reached the first junction, where the branch crossed another, he decided to change paths. The second caterpillar turned as well. Soon, there was a line of caterpillars, bumper to bumper, that flowed up one branch and onto another.

At the next junction, the leader made another decision and turned again. This was wise, as the new route led to fresh leaves and food. Again, the line turned. Back at home base, half of the original caterpillars still milled about, while the other half had formed a moving line that stretched over three feet.

In the midst of one of the lines was a tiny caterpillar. It was about half the size of the others and faced much disrespect. Unable to keep the same pace, the little one was constantly being pushed and passed. Bumped out of the way, he had to grasp the branch at an angle, giving way to the larger adversary. Once passed, the little one regained balance, only to be passed again by the next in line.

Finally, the little one reached the second junction. Tired of being pushed around, he saw a new path and took it. The one behind now had to choose which line to follow. Though he chose the common path, the next caterpillar did follow the little one, and soon there were two lines.

It wasn't long until the little one stopped. He had found fresh leaves as well. But there were not as many leaves on the second path as there were on the first, and soon there were many caterpillars turning around and trying to get back into the main line. As I left, I knew that all of the caterpillars were secure, as all paths led to survival. The tree they were on was covered with small budding leaves.

What can I read into these observations?

The leader took a random path. He (or she) simply began before the others. There were numerous branches stemming from the nest, but all of the caterpillars followed the same path.

Every caterpillar was both following and leading. The caterpillars at the end had no idea who or where the leader was. Choosing to emerge from the nest, you might as well go where everyone else is going.

Every caterpillar had a chance to be a leader. Any one of them could have begun the line. Every one of them could have turned at a junction. However, for that group of caterpillars only two made decisions. The first was an average caterpillar, similar to all of the others. The second was a little one, the runt of the litter. In the entire line, none were smaller. And yet the path of many came from the need of the runt to find a new way.

Even when they find food and grow, the caterpillars have no idea what will happen to them. Those not eaten by birds or other insects will one day wrap themselves in silk, and begin a transformation beyond imagination. Standing above the caterpillars, it was easy for me to determine the best path. I could not show them, so I simply had to observe. I knew that their survival was random, though individual choices could extend or shorten existence. Each caterpillar made a choice.

There is nothing in this world that we see that really has meaning. Events only have meaning when we choose to give them meaning. Our assumptions may be right or wrong, but the meanings we create express our choice of what to learn.

Transformation Exercises

1. Take a walk outside.

2. Observe what occurs around you.

3. Tell a story about something you saw.

Alter Ego

WHAT IS EGO? In some philosophies, the ego is an illusion, a self-created condition that causes us pain. Other philosophies consider the ego as the part of us that is most real. Some advisors tell us to eliminate ego, while others tell us to cherish it.

There are two conflicting and truthful statements about our species: We are all the same and we are all different. The ego is that part of ourselves that makes us unique. We identify ourselves as individuals and act in our own best interests. Ego is self-awareness, the aspect of ourselves that we identify with.

Much of our ego develops through training. Our self-esteem, gender identity, attitude and perceptions are all developed through experience and interaction. We evaluate all external influences by how they affect us. Often, our assumptions are incorrect and we apply meanings that are far from the truth. Sometimes we do things that are good for us; sometimes we harm ourselves. In either case, our ego stimulates us to take action.

In many eastern religions, the goal of meditation is to transcend the consciousness of ego, to separate from individuality and become one with the universe. Escape from the ego brings us into an existence of pure love and values, without judgment or anxiety. Living within ego is seen as the Buddhist equivalent of hell, an illusion dominated by appearances, opinions, and conditional love.

According to Sigmund Freud, the 'ego' is the level of consciousness that operates using the reality principle. The desires of the 'id' and the values of the 'superego' are managed in real time by the 'ego'. The 'ego' is often the cause of repression of urges or realization of guilt and fear, and is the part of us that we represent to the world.

Most of our thoughts are related to ourselves. We analyze our past, our future, our potential and our options. We think of others based on our interaction with them; what we said and what we heard. We survey our environment, determining how we can influence it, or if we need to protect ourselves. We gain or lose confidence, sometimes based on actual experience, sometimes based on illusions that we create.

Our ego gives us the desire to survive. Though many things are important to us, the preservation of existence is crucial. There may be instances where we are willing to risk or sacrifice our existence, such as protecting loved ones or participating in war. Other times, people risk their lives for thrill, or take their lives out of desperation. While ego is the root of our survival, it is also the root of our demise.

The ego obstructs the realization of oneness. We find it difficult to stop thinking about our current issues. All of our worries, anxieties, guilt, fears, and frustrations are driven by ego. Feelings of 'poor me' and 'nothing goes right' are egocentric, along with the expectations that we create. The more that we see ourselves as individuals, the more we identify what is lacking in our life.

On the other hand, ego also helps us realize joy. Success, accomplishment, inner peace, happiness, and love of life are often related to our current position as an individual. Much of our creative force occurs as a response to our desires. We want, so we act accordingly.

Suppose that we achieved an existence where ego was eliminated and all minds were linked. All people would act as one, with each individual simply a component of the mass. Any advantages gained by this evolution would be for naught, as none could appreciate it. Though most negative aspects of our society would be eliminated, the positive aspects of ego would also be denied.

The ego has a place in our lives. Without it we would think as one but be incapable of enjoying it. To be truly functional as individuals, we must operate within a state of ego, yet still be able to identify and separate those feelings that are dominated by ego. The ego is a wonderful part of our human character, though it often creates more pain than joy. Once we become aware of both the workings and trappings of ego, we are able to use it to our advantage.

Transformation Exercises

1. Go to a mirror and look yourself in the eye.

2. Tell yourself 'I love you, and everything that you are'.

3. Was the experience easy or difficult?

4. Describe how your ego has been an advantage.

5. Describe how your ego has been a disadvantage.

The Root of Polarity

POLARITY BEGINS WITH me and you. It continues into us and them, we and they, this side and that side. The journey begins when we cross the bridge of separation, and identify ourselves as unique individuals. Suddenly we are faced with choices and the requirement to make judgments in order to survive. In order to choose we must first differentiate. We become skilled at identifying variances.

The root of society comes down to the most basic choice, between good and bad. We all have an opinion and our opinions are unlimited. Everything that we are exposed to requires us to categorize, so we separate our world into likes, dislikes and neutral items. From the food we eat to the people we interact with, our choices can be identified by seeing what exists in our lives.

Now that we know how to differentiate, we become separated. In retaining a sense of self, we also create the reality that you are different than me. It is those differences that can lead to conflict. Strangely enough, while we realize that we are each separate individuals, it is the similarities that draw us together. We gather in groups or tribes or clubs or families, united by aspects that are common among us. You may find yourself in more than one group, linked by different common elements. In choosing which aspects of self are important to us, we bond with those that strengthen our connection.

The important thing to remember is that recognition of polarity involves training and choice. We notice differences that are important to us and overlook details that are not perceived as significant. To identify a polarity is common, since our entire world is formed of contrast. However, it is our reaction to each polarity that changes energy. If you think that something is very very good or very very bad, you will react differently than if you feel neutral.

Become aware of which polarities exist for you, how you react to them, and how they affect your environment. Begin with your greatest likes and dislikes, then work down to subtle reactions. As you begin to feel the changes in your energetic field upon the introduction of new stimuli, become aware of how you change physically, and what thoughts cross your mind. Once you learn how to do this without judgment, you will discover that everything is neutral until you put feelings into it.

Transformation Exercises

1. List three polarities that occurred in your life this week.

2. Evaluate your feelings about each extreme of the polarity.

3. Compare feelings between the three polarities and rank their energetic effect on your vibration.

One Way or Another

IN NATIVE AMERICAN mythology, there is a spiritual being called a 'Heyokah' (pronounced hey-OH-ka). A Heyokah is a person or spirit who does things backwards or opposite. He teaches people by testing beliefs and making them figure things out for themselves. By being contrary, the Heyokah reminds us that we are merely human beings and not to become too serious about ourselves. Similar to a 'devil's advocate', a contrary can be a difficult person to be around as they question our values. Being reminded that there is another way of perceiving things can be both frustrating and educational.

Everything has polarity. No matter what the topic, statements can be developed identifying positive or negative elements. The same goes for all discussions that are a matter of opinion or belief. Even if the majority of people accept the belief, it doesn't mean it is right. The definition of right and wrong can be as arbitrary as geographic location.

Cultural differences often provide the most extreme cases of polarity. Whenever you read the news and cringe, remember that the behavior we are so opposed to is acceptable in other societies. Eating dogs, expressing anger physically, or chopping the hands off thieves are all behaviors accepted in other parts of the world. While I am glad that I live in a culture that finds these actions despicable, it is important to remember that others can find weakness in our accepted lifestyles. Remember that any judgment you make is based on your own belief system.

Our individual morals and values have been influenced by our upbringing, our culture, and our experiences. Once a value is in place, you are likely to have it for life. Core beliefs resonate through our entire being and rarely change. While specific opinions may vary with time and information, the values you hold dearest are the same year after year. When your values are challenged, it is difficult to understand how anyone could believe otherwise. Your values define who you are and when they are disputed you may have to re-examine your beliefs.

A Heyokah reveals to people their limits and vulnerability, reminding others that the spirit is more powerful than the physical presence. Sometimes this is done through logic or aggression; other times it is done with humor. Laughter can break bonds, helping create growth in others. Fear can be diminished through laughter, for when we are smiling, the threat of danger seems reduced.

In other situations, anger brings our values to the surface. I had a friend who represented one aspect of Heyokah. He loved to argue and would usually take an opposing view just to enrage people. He was very outspoken and could find alternatives to anything. If you liked the red team, he would pick the blue team; if you said yes he would say no. Political and value discussions were his specialties, and no matter how much you believed in your perspective, he could always find an alternative argument. This often drove people crazy.

What was most interesting in observing my friend was seeing how easily he could get a reaction. By thinking in opposites, he would reveal to people the weakness of their position. Sometimes this revelation served to change values, while other times the questions raised caused people to believe even more firmly in their ideals.

On one Election Day where a particular party was heavily favored, my friend boldly announced to the crowd that the main opponent would win the election. Of course heavy debate ensued and the energy in the room completely shifted. Shortly afterwards I met my friend at the bar, and he laughed as he stated 'I didn't even vote!'

The next time that you firmly think to yourself 'Yes it is!' think of someone in the background saying 'No, it isn't'. When you are absolutely sure you are right, imagine what someone may say to prove that you are wrong. Everything you see, everything you say, everything you think and everything you do can be perceived in one way or another. May you find alternatives in your life.

Transformational Exercises

1. What three personal values do you believe in most passionately?

2. Identify why you think these beliefs are correct.

3. Make an argument to defend why the opposite values may be correct.

Have a NICE Day!

As our planet undergoes vibrational shifts, many people are experiencing heightened awareness. For some, personal issues have come to the surface, and we continue our work of healing. It is a time when people can release old issues and move into a new vibration. It is a time when we can have direct impact on our growth, creating a new future for ourselves.

In our heightened vibration, old memories and feelings are shaken to the surface. People from your past may have come back into your life, or the characteristics of new acquaintances may remind you of someone. Old scenes are triggered, and we become aware of how certain feelings have developed. Often, we realize how deeply affected we are by certain memories and beliefs.

When an old memory returns, there are likely emotions attached. Sometimes the emotion is joyous and sometimes it is painful. There may be memories that have been repressed or ignored because they are too painful to deal with, or other memories whose flavor has changed with time. Some recollections involve incredible detail, enough for us to write a script or paint a picture. At either a conscious or subconscious level, memories are utilized to awaken emotions.

We tend to relive certain memories, recreating feelings and strengthening the neural pathways that support the story. Familiar pathways become like well-worn grooves, continually coaxing thoughts in the same direction. The way that we think becomes habit and our responses become easily triggered. Situations and experiences are compared to previous encounters and we fall into patterns.

If we understand how the mind works, we can make a conscious effort to improve our thought patterns. Altering our thoughts will alter our emotions, not with the intention of eliminating emotion, but with the intention of re-directing emotions and using them as an important and useful part of our existence. We should not be afraid to feel, but neither should we be trapped in negativity or stagnation. When emotions and beliefs hold back our progress, it becomes time to release and move forward the NICE way.

NICE stands for Neurally Integrated Consciousness Expansion. The NICE way implies using intentional thoughts and behavioral training to expand consciousness beyond its current levels. By raising awareness to the level where thought patterns can be recognized, it becomes possible to make choices and encourage the creation of different neural pathways. Each time you consciously create thoughts with positive outcome, you increase the chances of that neural path occurring again.

The key element of thought recognition is to separate now from then·

Often we recall memories that awaken feelings. A particular event or circumstance may have had great impact on our life. Recalling the memory of the event can directly affect our feelings. It is important to recognize that these feelings have been invoked by thoughts. It is always possible to stop thinking about the stimulating event and return to a more neutral space. By experimenting with meditation and contemplation of memories, it is possible to resolve old conflicts and release old issues.

It is possible to exist in a heightened state of awareness. It is possible to create a happy, joyous and creative existence. Why settle for less? Have a NICE day!

Transformational Exercises

1. Identify three old memories that still surface every now and then.

2. Write down the story of that memory.

3. What feelings are identified by each memory?

4. If there are memories that produce undesired feelings, identify a related story or event that leads to positive feelings. For example, if you have a depressing memory related to a certain place, identify a happy memory in the same or similar place.

The Man on the Beach

EVERY DAY, THE man on the beach ate fruit. It was what kept him alive. And yet the man on the beach did not grow the fruit. It was there for the picking and he picked it.

The man who grew the fruit knew about this and was unsure what to do. There really was lots of fruit and the man on the beach ate less than the amount thrown away as spoiled goods. But what really irked the man who grew the fruit was the fact that the man on the beach did nothing.

Growing fruit requires effort. While fruits will grow wildly, the practice of farming manages to increase production greatly. Farming requires investment and farming requires work. Lots of work.

One day, the man who grew the fruit approached the man on the beach and sat beside him.

'Why do you do nothing but sit on the beach?'

'I am here to meditate'

'What do you meditate about?'

'I visualize myself on a beach, the sun shining and the waves gently rolling to the shore. Stretched behind me are acres and acres of fresh fruit, more than I could ever eat in my lifetime.'

'I grow the fruit for you', stated the man who grew the fruit.

'You are the farmer?' asked the man who lived on the beach. The farmer nodded in reply.

'Before you were here, there was fruit growing wildly, more than I could possibly eat in a lifetime. Now that you are here, there is fruit for many. I visualized not just enough for me but enough for many.'

'What did you visualize about me?' asked the farmer.

'A man of spirit, one who realizes the universal benefits of sharing. Allowing things to grow, allowing abundance to occur.'

The farmer stood up, smiled and walked back to the farm. He visualized abundance and there was.

Transformation Exercises

1. What are your feelings about the man on the beach?

2. Do you believe that you have to work to survive?

3. Describe your ideal 'getaway' vacation.

Mindset

WHEN YOU WAKE up in the morning, what are the first thoughts that come to your mind? Do you immediately recall dreams and review them in an awakened state? Do tasks and duties come to mind? Or do you simply have a morning routine, completed sequentially without much thought?

The first thoughts that come to your mind in the morning may be related to your last thoughts from the previous night. If you were concerned or worried about something as you closed your eyes, those feelings may regenerate early in your day. If you are feeling negative about aspects of your life, how long does it take for those feelings to join you in the morning?

As your day progresses, you mold into your persona. Who you are today is influenced by who you were yesterday. People tend to habitually follow patterns that define experiences. We tend to do the same things in the same way and to have the same thoughts and feelings day after day.

It is often in retrospect that we realize we have changed. Years ago, after experiencing frequent headaches for years, I suddenly realized that I had not experienced pain for six months. Only when I was comfortably in my new vibration could I look back and understand why I didn't get headaches anymore. I realized that my pain was directly related to my way of thinking and my way of being. As a cure for my headaches, I had changed lifestyles and was much happier.

While it is often easy to recognize change after it has happened, we have more power than we realize. Change comes from within, and by consciously redirecting your energy to become who you want to be, success is only a matter of time.

The key to mindset is to recognize that your thoughts directly influence your feelings, and to move yourself in the direction that you really want to go. Begin by recognizing that in the morning, each day starts fresh, and if you decide to feel positive about yourself and your life, the day unfolds in a much more pleasant manner.

Transformation Exercises

1. Identify a characteristic or issue that you no longer have.

2. How did you change to overcome the issue?

3. Was the change easy or difficult? How could it have been easier?

4. Identify your next target for change.

UR NO 1

As I SAT in my car waiting for a red light to turn green, I noticed the license plate of the car in front of me. UR NO 1. You are no-one. Then I realized that it could also be read a different way. You are number one. The license plate reflected both ends of the spectrum of ego. When you first read the title of this article, which pronunciation did you see? Recognize that what you perceive reflects what is within.

The ego has a delicate balance and self-esteem is often tested. Though we would like to control our environment, results seem to have limitations. Things don't always go the way that we desire. As the center of our own universe, each of us looks for personal gratification. Though many realize that fulfillment comes from within, often our personal condition is reflected by the world around us.

As humanity grows spiritually, we move towards oneness. We recognize that we are all part of the same energy field, in which each person is special and worthy and we are fully interdependent. However, if everyone is special, than no-one is. If equality is truly reached, then no-one has an advantage or disadvantage. Everything would be available for everyone. We would all be the same.

Somehow, I don't think sameness is the target of oneness. The glory of humanity shines brightest with the unique contribution of individuals. While some have moved towards darkness, the history of humanity reveals the special creations of many unique souls. Through activities such as art, music, construction, science, and philosophy, people have added their special flavor to the sum total of human creation. Humanity is improved by a simple moment of joy or compassion by those who have the courage to help others shine.

If you are no-one, then your uniqueness blends with everyone else, and you are part of the crowd. If you are number one, then you are special above everyone else. The paradox of existence is that both perceptions are true. If you only believe in one extreme or the other, an imbalance is created. If you are no-one, the ego can be bruised, and depression can set in. If you are number one, then sharing becomes less important, and others may suffer due to your self-centeredness.

As no-one, you have no responsibilities. As number one, you carry the weight of the world on your shoulders. The challenge of the new reality is to be able to exist in both places at once, expressing your unique and special presence as an equal part of the whole.

Transformation Exercises

1. Think of someone you hold in high esteem. What makes this person unique and special? In which ways is this person just like everyone else?

2. Think of someone that you know, who doesn't play a major role in your life. What makes this person unique and special? In which ways is this person just like everyone else?

Vibration and Energy

'It is possible to anticipate coming changes in any human field by monitoring the insights that are finding their way into expression at the creative edge of human thought.'

Ken Carey, The Third Millenium, 1991

What A Feeling

HAVE YOU EVER been in a situation where you know that the right answer is wrong, or that the wrong answer is right? Everything that you know tells you to make one decision, yet you are compelled to act differently. You fear the outcome, yet know if you make the expected choice, it just isn't right for you.

Many of us have been trained to think logically. When an issue presents itself, we think through the options and alternatives, identifying risks and solutions until we decide on an approach. Step by step, we compare the situation to previous experiences and consider what others may have done in similar circumstances. Using logic, everything makes sense.

What do we do if there is missing information? If logic fails to support a decision, we fill in the gaps with educated guesses. Our perceptions are based on our senses, what we can see and feel and remember, or what someone else has reported as a definite outcome. Yet somehow, when we really need to, we make decisions that defy logic.

Our terminology and language pay tribute to our intuitive ability. People can 'have a gut feeling' or 'follow their heart'. A decision can 'feel right' or 'look good'. The phrase 'women's intuition' is part of our common speech and recognizes the innate ability of females to determine a course of action based not on logic but emotion. Men often ridicule women about their decision-making, yet more often than not women are correct. No matter how much something makes sense, if it doesn't feel right it shouldn't be done.

What do we mean when we speak of a gut feeling? Is it simply a bias towards a certain outcome, a tendency to prefer one choice to another, or is there an actual physical reaction based on our internal knowledge? Sometimes when we consider our options, we can actually feel sensations in our chest and belly. As we increase our awareness and connect with our senses, we can decide the proper course of action based upon our feelings.

When advertising popularized the philosophy 'If it feels good, do it', there was a belief that the statement was hedonistic, an attempt to receive physical reward and pleasure. However, we have within us the ability to decide based purely on emotional reaction. Like a dowsing stick, our gut feeling can help us choose the right path. When we add physical sensations to mental logic, we increase our ability to determine the proper course of action.

Learning to guide your life by feelings is not as simple as reacting emotionally. Emotions can be contrived, created by our perception of a situation. Emotions tend to follow our training and previous experiences, so that we avoid pain and chase pleasure. Unfortunately, our deductions may have been wrong. The feelings may be the result of fear, self-esteem, or nervousness. It is necessary to determine if your reaction to stimuli is based on truth or on training.

In some cases, intuitive thought is just a lucky guess. Since we live in a linear world, we usually cannot know the outcome of a different path. Perhaps there was more than one correct choice, or perhaps all choices would have led to the same result. It is only in retrospect that we can determine whether a choice was a mistake. Even then, choices that cause short-term difficulty can lead to ultimate good.

Intuition can be immediate and clear. The concept of luminosity encourages people to follow their awareness. Luminosity occurs when you look at a wall full of books and one stands out, or when you look into a crowd of people and immediately focus on one person. Somehow, we are drawn to something without knowing the reason. When we follow these intuitive feelings, we are often rewarded with knowledge, information, or inspiration.

In a society that teaches its young to think logically, it is difficult to forego factual analysis. When intuition, coincidence, luminosity, and feelings become apparent, we are often put at conflict with our logical mind. Learn to increase your awareness and allow the mysterious guidance of the universe to enter your perception. Not everything is logical.

Transformational Exercises

1. List the past few decisions that you have made. Determine whether they were made logically or intuitively.

2. Describe how you felt when you made an intuitive decision.

3. Become aware of how you feel when you are stressed, confident, happy or angry.

Teach the World to Sing

IF YOU WERE a tuning fork, what note would you be?

Would you hum like the harp of an angel, or bleat like a rusty trombone?

All sound is vibration, and all vibration is energy. The sounds that we hear are caused by vibration, such as the plucking of a guitar string, the hum of an engine, or the resonance of the vocal chords. Sound is created through a transfer of energy, causing a vibration of the eardrum. We perceive this vibration as sound.

There are other types of vibration that we perceive, though we don't hear them. We feel the vibration of an underground train, we feel the heat of the sun, we the feel the presence of someone in the room even if the lights are out.

Each of us vibrates with energy, and each of us emits a tone. We vibrate with the energy that we choose; we also vibrate with the energy on which we are focused. When you are vibrating in a specific way, then the vibrations that you are exposed to may have a greater or lesser effect. Though we can't hear the vibration that we are emitting, we can sense it. Our language speaks of this capability.

I walked into the party and the room was buzzing with energy.
He set the tone for the meeting.
I'm in tune.

When vibrations fit together in a pleasing way, it is called harmony. Harmony is the combination of musical notes in a chord, in a pleasing or congruent manner. Harmony can be of color as well as music, for the colors we perceive are simply the vibration of light waves. Harmony creates internal calm and tranquility.

If we all vibrated in harmony, it would be beautiful, like the chords of a church organ. The vibration of sound that we currently create is static, with only some souls in unison. However, as the number of souls vibrating in harmony increases, the song becomes louder and easier to follow. Ultimately, the hum created by a planet in harmony would be a single note, pure and easy and beautiful.

Remember the old slogan from Coke™? "I'd like to teach the world to sing in perfect harmony." Think about the beauty of all people in tune, vibrating in harmony around the world. Then take your thoughts further. Think of harmony in the entire universe.

Uni-verse. One song. A perfect harmonious chord.

How does one go about tuning their vibration? First, don't spend your time thinking about yesterday, or tomorrow, or what you don't have, or what someone did to you, or what you should have done. Instead, think about now, or don't think at all. Simply enjoy the moment.

Secondly, your vibration follows your focus. If you focus on anger, then you will vibrate anger. If you focus on lacking, then you will vibrate lacking, and that is what you will experience. Instead, focus on love, joy, and acceptance. Accept your world as it is, find joy in everything, and feel a deep, accepting love for everyone and everything in your path. Vibrate love and this is what you will experience.

How we feel is reflected in our vibration. How we vibrate is reflected in how we feel. Imagine how you feel when you are in a state of joy or happiness. Imagine how that feeling can change into depression or sadness. You resonate with different energy in each of these emotional states. It is possible to change your vibration when you identify how you want to feel. By comparing to past experiences that fit your desired vibration, it is simpler to adjust your energy to the state that you desire.

Love is the vibration to which we should all aim; pure simple unconditional love; of yourself, of your world, and of everything in it. It is not a matter of striving, as effort can make the vibration stale and rigid. Instead, one should simply allow oneself to vibrate in a certain way, to tend towards a certain type of vibration. In doing so, we become more harmonically connected with that vibration, and its achievement becomes a certainty.

Transformational Exercises

1. Focus on your breathing, and move into a meditative state.

2. Recall a past experience that was pleasant. Check in with your body to see how each area feels.

3. Recall a past experience that was unpleasant. Again, check in and analyze your feelings.

4. Describe how you were able to alter the way you felt by altering your thoughts.

See the Light

A FIELD OF energy surrounds the human body. Some people perceive this field as light and identify it as an aura. People with High Sensory Perception (HSP) are capable of diagnosing mood, personality, and health-related issues through the reading of the aura.

The first time that I saw a human aura was at a meeting. I was watching a man speak at the front of the room and began to see a bright blue glow surrounding his head. Though the thin glow was distinct, I thought there was something wrong with my eyes. Perhaps it was the fluorescent lights that were causing me to focus incorrectly, or perhaps my eyes were just tired.

When the next speaker got up, I could see a glow around her as well. As she moved her head, a thick trail of blue light remained behind for an instant, and then followed her. That night, those were the only two people around whom I could see this glow. I could not ignore the fact that I had seen something, but I couldn't explain it.

When I got home, I started to document my experience, and realized something very important. I had seen a glow around two people, and each was different. If it were just a trick of the light, the glow would have been the same. If it were a problem with my eyes, the glow would have been the same. I had seen auras for the first time.

Since then, I have seen the human aura countless times. I do not see them all of the time. If I happen to tell someone about this ability, they usually ask if I can see their aura. For me, it doesn't happen that easily. I am still learning how to turn this ability on and off.

Sometimes it takes me by surprise. One day, a young woman came up behind me and called my name. When I turned around to look at her, I saw her surrounded by a distinct bluish glow, colored like a gas flame. Though I was impressed, I didn't say anything about it. To me, it is still not socially acceptable to turn to someone and tell them that you can see their aura.

Seeing the aura is a trainable skill. I attended a course on seeing auras offered by Mark Smith. At the beginning of the class, he asked how many people had seen auras previously. I was one of five who said yes. The rest of the class of sixty had not. At the end of the class, he asked again. Only five people remained who had not seen the aura that night.

Do you remember seeing 3-Dimensional pictures on calendars or posters? The picture is a mass of color, something like a mural, with many small shapes repeated. However, as you stare at it, a form becomes visible. Eventually, in the mass of color you can very clearly see a butterfly, a tree, or another shape. In order to see the shape, you must change the way that you focus your eyes. Seeing auras is also a result of changing focus.

Normally, we tend to look at the physical presence. When we look at the person, we tend to look them in the eye (or surreptitiously look at their body). When you look at a physical object, you are actually seeing a reflection of light from that person or object. Instead, you must see through the reflection to see the energy radiated. This is accomplished by focusing on a point behind your subject.

It is not always easy to do. When I try hard to see an aura, I often cannot. Do not be disappointed if you try and try and cannot see them. Simply relax your eyes and accept that auras exist. Sooner or later they will begin to appear.

The human aura is a reflection of who the person is and what they are feeling. People emanate different auras at different times. An aura is like a portrait and these portraits appear in color. Some people can perceive your aura, visually, emotionally, or by touch.

Auras are real. I can see the light. So can you.

Transformational Exercises

1. Are you aware of your ability to see auras?

2. How does your belief system affect what you see?

3. Practice seeing auras on plants, animals, and humans.

The Real Body Language

THE FIELD OF energy surrounding your body interacts directly with other people. Though many people cannot see the human aura, we can all perceive it. The concept of body language, described as visual in nature, is actually a representation of the energy we are emitting. The real body language has a physical as well as a psychological explanation.

While being trained to see auras, I was exposed to the concept of aura interaction. Pairs of people were put at the front of the room for the students to observe. First, two men stood face to face, and while I could see both of their auras, there was a distinct gap between them. Their auras moved back to avoid contact. Next, two women got up, and their auras did not retract. Instead, the fields of light seemed to mingle.

A young man and woman got up in front of the class and faced each other. While her aura remained quite stable, his aura noticeably expanded towards her. When we want to get closer to someone, we radiate a different type of energy.

Finally, an older married couple got up and faced each other. Their auras were different colors. His was blue and hers was yellow. The colors intermingled to a greenish hue between them. What I found most remarkable were the lines that I could see. There were dark lines of purple light, about an inch thick, extending from forehead to forehead, throat to throat, chest to chest. I could quite distinctly see lines of energy connecting the two people.

The lines of energy that I could see corresponded directly with their chakras. Chakras are points in the body where energy moves in a vortex. There are seven major chakras, located at the groin, pelvis, solar plexus, heart, throat, brow, and scalp. The energy of each chakra forms into a shape like a small tornado, with the base point emanating from the body and opening like a funnel. There are funnels of energy both front and back.

When people are communicating, they turn towards each other. The body language of a fully open stance is not just symbolic. It is the opening of the chakras to each other. Crossing arms over the chest blocks the energy from that particular chakra. When you are in a meeting, do you sit with an arm in front of your chest? While this position may seem to be most comfortable, it serves to prevent connection or sharing of energy with the person across from you. Or at least, you do not want to share heart chakra energy.

When you have close interaction with someone, the energy from your chakras extends to join with the corresponding point on the other person. An open stance, face to face, allows full connection of aura energy. Any move away from the open stance reduces the connection.

When we are speaking with someone at close range, we often begin the conversation with our bodies at a slight angle. As the conversation continues, and as closeness grows, we turn to face the other squarely. This has the effect of lining up the chakras, allowing a free flow of energy.

Various postures that we take either enhance or reduce energetic connection. Someone who stands with arms crossed in front is not only presenting a visual image of protection; he is actually covering the heart chakra, stopping the other's energy from connecting. A person resting his chin on his hand also blocks connection of the energy at the throat.

The connection of eyes is one of the main catalysts in allowing energy bonding to occur.

We are all aware of eye contact. When you look at someone across the room, and they are staring back at you, it is easy to tell if they are looking at you or at someone beside you. This is because an energetic bond has been created. When we avert our eyes, we are denying the connection.

Understanding the body as energy can be difficult. We are physical beings, and often cannot accept things that we cannot see and prove. Nevertheless, our aura has a direct influence on interaction with others. We communicate with our energy and others perceive it. Some people are consciously aware of your energy field, while others simply feel its effects. Increase your awareness and discover a new level of perception.

Transformational Exercises

1. Move your hands slowly together without touching, and again in front of your face. Can you sense the energy field?

2. Working with a partner, close your eyes and let your partner move his/her hand close to you without touching. Become aware of the energy field.

3. Observe how other people interact, and analyze their body language using the chakra-interaction model.

Good Vibrations

WITHIN THE ENGLISH language, common statements are often closer to the truth than we currently understand. When people are 'connected', the definition implies that there is a bond or understanding between individuals. What many fail to notice is that there is an actual energetic connection that takes place in a trusting relationship. The connection that occurs joins people at the chakra points and can actually be seen by those open enough to witness the aura in action.

When people speak 'from the heart', our belief is that they are telling us what they truly believe. What is also happening is that the heart chakra is opening and connecting. While one can 'lie through the teeth', it is impossible for the energy field to mislead. If you are attempting to deceive, another who is aware can 'see it in your eyes'.

Similarly, one who 'keeps their feet on the ground' is more solid than one whose 'head is in the clouds'. The connection to the earth, referred to in healing and martial arts as 'grounding', is a necessary part of staying centered, focused and in the moment. The spiritual connection, which occurs through the crown chakra at the top of the head, tends to make one more ethereal. One who feels happy and positive radiates more energy, and is said to be 'glowing', while one feeling sluggish and depressed looks rather 'pale'. When people are blessed with insight or spiritual capabilities beyond the common person, they are said to be in a 'higher vibration'. There is more to this than 'meets the eye'.

In experiments performed at UCLA by Professor Valerie Hunt, the human energy field was analyzed using technologies similar to the electroencephalograph (EEG, which measures the strength and frequency of the brain's energy), and the electrocardiograph (EKG, which measures the electrical activity of the heart). While many question the presence of a human aura they cannot see, they openly accept the application of medical science to the electromagnetic field of the body, though most cannot pronounce more than the acronyms.

Average energetic frequencies have been identified to assist physicians in their diagnoses. The frequency of the brain normally resonates between zero and one hundred cycles per second (cps), with the standard vibration between 0 and 30 cps. The muscles have higher frequencies, achieving levels up to 225 cps, while the heart resonates at a maximum of 250 cps. Though the resonance of the heart, brain or muscles can reduce to zero during rest or illness, the resonance of the physical body rarely exceeds the stated maximums.

Interesting results were discovered when measurements were taken of the energy field surrounding the body. While the resonance of the body is relatively low, the resonance of the aura can achieve much higher levels. When the subject was focused on the material world, the resonance of the aura barely exceeded 250 cps. However, when the subject began to meditate, pray, or enter psychic or healing mode, the energetic resonance began to rise.

People with basic psychic or healing abilities created a resonance between 400 and 800 cps. Advanced healers, or those with trance channeling psychic abilities, resonated at levels ranging from 800 to 900 cps. Extremely powerful mystics were measured at much greater levels, with some individuals creating an energetic resonance in excess of 200,000 cps! Those capable of an advanced state are truly at a higher vibration.

In further experiments, it was discovered that those who practiced meditation on a regular basis were capable of much greater vibration and telekinetic ability. Contact with the unconscious, or higher self, can enhance ones capabilities. Most of those who practice meditation or spiritual work understand that 'connection to source' takes us to a higher level, but now it can be proven scientifically.

While it is possible to enhance your healing and psychic abilities through practiced study and meditation, the goal of increased vibration should not be your only focus. Paired with the physical changes are spiritual growth, personal development, and deeper compassion and love for all of mankind. Good vibrations lead to personal healing, greater insight, and enhanced capabilities. In addition, through sharing and interaction, your higher vibration influences others on both a conscious and energetic level.

Transformation Exercises

1. Throughout your day, make a list of phrases that people commonly use.

2. Identify how meanings would change if the phrases were taken literally.

3. Become aware of your personal vibration while calm and at rest.

4. Compare your vibration during different experiences to how you felt while calm.

Skills of Perception

MANY PEOPLE DO not have good listening skills. They are more concerned about getting across their point of view than actually communicating. They have not considered learning to read body language, aura, and vocal intonation. However, I have learned that increased awareness during interaction becomes an advantage.

By moving into a position of balance and receptivity, it becomes evident that individuals (and groups!) communicate with much more than words. By understanding someone's true feelings and intentions, it becomes easier to move towards a common agreement.

How this advantage is used is up to the individual. Like any skill, high perceptive capabilities can be used with positive or negative intent. As our species evolves, there will be those capable of manipulating the unaware. There is much evidence of that already.

As people grow in awareness, they become more difficult to manipulate. When you understand energetic interaction, you become aware of the attempts of others to influence your own energy. You then discover that it is totally your decision whether to comply or not. Though there may be external interaction, as an energetic being you choose your vibration.

When we reach a critical mass of awareness, the higher level of interaction will be less of a weapon and more an enhanced method of communication, nearing telepathy. Once we learn how to interact in ways that create positive growth for all involved, we will begin to learn about the power that we hold as a species.

Transformation Exercises

1. Sit alone in a public place and watch the behavior of others.

2. When in one-on-one communication, maintain awareness.

3. When in group communication, spend time listening rather than speaking or thinking about your next speech.

Challenging Thoughts

MANKIND IS AT a turning point, and while some believe that change depends on politics and war, lightworkers intend on changing the world at a molecular level. There is more to being a lightworker than simply being nice to people. By being in a state of harmony, a physical being can help pull others towards that harmonious state.

Recent scientific experiments have revealed that people (and all living creatures) actually emit light particles, identified on some scales as light radiation. While the light is so faint that it can barely be seen, there are some whose perceptive abilities have advanced far enough to see the human aura.

There is also more to vibration than simply being in a positive state of mind. There is an actual molecular signature that each cell in our body creates, and this signature vibration is unique to every individual. While we can enhance our vibration through soul work and positive intent, the base vibration is directly dependent upon coding that resides in our DNA.

Of course, many people refuse to believe in auras or vibration or soul. It is simpler to see the world as external and to believe that reality depends on our ability to touch and feel something. Our egos take over and we are sure that information that comes through our senses must be correct. Any vision that borders on etheric must be superstitious hogwash, and though millions believe in angels and demons, surprisingly few are willing to admit that there is a universal plan for us all.

As we begin to redefine reality, new capabilities come to the human species. By understanding vibration and how it affects our personal health, we learn how to become whole, and how to help our entire body vibrate in ordered unison. Illness can be directly related to vibrational issues, either in our belief system or in specific parts of our body. Communication also occurs at a molecular and vibrational level. Those who are capable of holding a steady tune will have more influence than those whose output is scattered and incoherent.

We know that all physical things are made of molecules. We also know that all molecules are formed of little pieces of energy that vibrate at a specific resonance. Since these statements have been scientifically proven, is it so impossible to believe that we may have influence over this energy, beyond our current knowledge and beliefs?

Transformation Exercises

1. What are your beliefs about auras and energetic vibration?

2. What aspects of your vibration do you feel in control of?

3. What aspects of your vibration require focus?

Understanding Energy

THE HUMAN SPECIES is evolving. The evolution first takes place at an energetic level, and then moves to intellectual and spiritual levels. When we begin to comprehend who we are and what we are capable of, things will change. The physical reality in which we reside is dependent upon certain barriers and rules that we have absorbed as common beliefs. However, once these barriers are broken, things will never be the same.

We begin to understand our world when we comprehend energy and how it works. Everything that is material consists of tiny atoms. Each atom consists of small masses of energy. The atoms bond together according to a natural structure. As the movement of the atoms slows down an object is formed. Though we can touch and feel physical objects, they ultimately have no more substance than anything else.

In the same way, our bodies are formed of atoms that are structured through the programming of our DNA. When perceived as a field of energy, the body takes on new meaning. When aura and chakras are understood and accepted, they can be manipulated through intent. Many health issues related to energy blockages can be overcome. Eventually identification of energy imbalances becomes the key element of self-healing.

Once we begin to understand ourselves as fields of energy massed into human form, we can then observe behavior in others that ratifies our beliefs. The science of body language is greatly enhanced by taking an energetic viewpoint. Understanding how auras and chakras interact reveals new aspects of human communication. Being able to see and feel the protective barriers that people form allows one to adapt and ease their tension energetically. When one is willing to adjust energy to assist another, the other usually relaxes into the merger.

By perceiving everything as energy, you become better able to work with yourself and those around you. Combining energy in pairs or groups becomes commonplace. It takes a certain way of being to allow your energy to merge with others, to enhance both theirs and your own energy, and yet to still retain your individual essence and power. You must trust yourself, and then trust the others. Your agenda should be not of control but instead group enhancement, contributing energy to the benefit of all.

Transformation Exercises

1. Do an evaluation of your energy field, and adjust where necessary.

2. Identify areas of energy blockage and release.

3. Practice perceiving other people as beings of energy.

Sweet Harmony

WHEN WE ARE happy and joyous, we vibrate in rhythm with the pulse of the earth. Our energy is attuned, and our harmonious existence increases our power. When we are depressed and sad, we are not in vibration with the earth. Our energy feels different. When we are not connected with the universe, we seek the energy of others to supplement our own.

To be in harmonious existence becomes natural as we feel it. Once we have been there, it is always possible to get back. The trick is to remain in vibration as long as you can, to stay in that place of perfection throughout your waking and sleeping life. Our tendency is to feel perfection only momentarily, and then to let it go. The flash of love, the quick exuberance of joy that strikes us and lights us up, is a blessed moment that emphasizes what we could be. Then, as quick as it comes, the flash fades away. Our thoughts distract us and the moment is lost.

Understanding your own vibration is key to personal growth. By realizing that your thoughts and activities directly affect your energy field, you can alter behavior to create the persona that pleases you most. Do you wish to be in harmony, or do you prefer to draw energy from others? Do you shine with the pleasure of life, or do you exude anxiety? What message does your light carry? How does it influence others?

There is nothing that is not within our power. We are great spirits in a transient universe, and create the world around us. Our greatest strength comes from being in harmonious resonance with our planet, which itself is in tune with the galaxy and the universe. By tuning in with the planetary vibration, we give it strength and carry the song to those around us. Our own resonance grows exponentially as we hum the song of life. Our drumbeat merges with others carrying the same rhythm and the message is passed.

If you were a tuning fork, what note would you be? Be aware of the mood and energy that you are emitting, and then adjust, sinking back into the relaxation of peaceful existence. There is a distinct feel to being in harmony. Harmony is something anyone can achieve regardless of state or condition. Just for the moment, become a balanced source of energy, and think not of past or future. Just be. Learn how to manage your energy, and drum with the earth. As you move into resonance, the effect is beyond your imagination. The world can be changed and it begins with you.

Transformation Exercises

1. Sit in peace and joy.

2. Balance your internal self.

3. Feel the resonance of the earth.

4. See the beauty around you.

Conscious Vibration

WHAT IS REALITY? We look through our eyes to see the world, and assume that everything is real. We read the news, listen to stories, watch television and believe that we understand the whole picture. Our expectations are based on belief systems. We tend to see what we expect. We think that our external world is beyond our control, and yet we really know within that we are omnipotent. As awareness increases, we realize that the world shakes with vibrational change, and each of us can play a role in the creation of a new future for mankind.

Power is usually diminished through direct confrontation. When one goes head to head with a giant, the giant usually wins. But by approaching the confrontation in an unexpected manner, victory is within our grasp. While some attempt to change the world with anger and violence, true lightworkers are changing the world at a vibrational level. By simply existing, and resonating truth and light, each lightworker influences the world. As our numbers grow, love and awareness grow exponentially, and the shift strengthens. Victory comes through serenity and peaceful enlightenment is the reward.

Whenever a lightworker exists in a condition of balance, the radiation of energy is increased. It is within ourselves that we find strength, and the strength of vibration is enhanced as we settle into joy. By opening our energy conduits and shifting into our power, our energy field is enhanced. The enhanced field is noticeable by those who are aware, yet still influences those who are not. The simple act of walking through a crowd with an enhanced energy field is enough to initiate change.

The world is changing, and the old guard of three-dimensional thinking battles for position. Governments and institutions take drastic measures to enforce their reality, desperately aware of crumbling from within. Those who have reached fifth-dimensional awareness smile peacefully, realizing that the energy of consciousness is more powerful than any weapon. Eliminate fear, radiate love, and remain aware of your power. Be conscious of each shift within your energy. Learn how to balance and expand your field. Be confident in your vibration and watch the world around you begin to change.

Transformation Exercises

1. Move your energy into a vibration of harmonious balance.

2. Sit in a public place and maintain your balance.

3. Experiment with your energy as you move around or sit in different locations.

Pass It On

WHAT A WONDERFUL time to be alive. As we learn about the power of our creative force, we set intention to make the world a better place. The contrast of what we don't want helps us direct our future and the potential is glorious. We live on a beautiful planet, with the ability to support billions of people, each with a comfortable life and creative future. We have the heat from the sun, the fertility of the earth, food from land and ocean and a sustainable bio-system. We could be living in paradise.

We have reached a point where technology connects us all. Unless we choose to isolate, the news of the world is always in front of us. We see and read and hear about all the bad things and believe that the world cannot be saved. We often believe that we can't make a difference. But we can.

It is all about vibration. When a person vibrates love and joy and peace and harmony, the world benefits. The benefit can have a direct effect, when an interaction passes joy to someone else. A smile may reverberate throughout the day and the person you smiled at may then choose to smile instead of frown. As that person continues to smile, many more people may be influenced, and the joy grows. Frowns and anger can also be passed along. It is important to remain aware of your vibration as you interact with others.

One of the most challenging aspects in shifting vibration is trust. The future is unknown and uncontrollable, and while we may attempt to influence, we are not in control. Like a surfer riding the waves, we can only steer and attempt to maintain balance. By learning to trust, we relax and the ride becomes easier. If we develop stress, tension and anxiety, we lose our balance and tend to fall.

This is not to say that there are not challenges. We are pulled in many directions, reminded of fears and memories and expectations. It takes discipline to remain in a harmonious vibration and perpetual refocusing may be required. Throughout the day, I will check in with myself, separating from the world for a brief moment to see where I am and what I am feeling. I can then decide which direction to take my vibration. You can too. Be joyous, be happy, and be at peace, and the world will come along with you.

Transformation Exercises

1. Practice 'checking in' throughout your day.

2. If stressful situations arise, check in before reacting.

3. When analyzing situations that have already occurred, check in before recalling the details.

Living in the Fifth Dimension

FOR MANY PEOPLE, reality is defined as a three-dimensional experience. The physical world can be measured by height, width and depth, and includes anything that can be perceived through physical senses. Each component of physical reality is seen as separate from ourselves, and each item has its own characteristics. While we have direct influence on the third dimension, change involves applying force. We can lift, move, stretch, bend, break or consume third-dimensional objects within the limitations of our physical power.

Recognition of the fourth dimension adds the factor of time. While our direct experiences always involve the phase of 'now', it is possible to measure changes over time. We can remember events that happened before 'now', and anticipate events that happen after 'now'. We can alter our behavior in the current 'now' to potentially change the future 'now'. While the movement of time is consistent, our perceptions can change its value. We are all familiar with the slow movement of time while we wait for someone, or the quick passing of time when we are having fun.

The next step is recognition of the fifth dimension, in which thought and energy directly influence our environment. Research reveals many sources that address the concepts of quantum reality and the recognition that all matter is really condensed energy. An interesting study is the work of Dr. Masuro Emoto, whose book 'The Hidden Messages in Water' reveals that thoughts can change the molecular form of water.

When water is exposed to thoughts such as 'love' and 'peace' and then frozen, it crystallizes into beautiful symmetrical snowflake shapes. When the same water is exposed to thoughts such as 'hatred' or 'anger', it crystallizes into muddled disorganized shapes. Unlikely as it may sound, our feelings directly influence the structure of water molecules. Since the human body consists mostly of water, there is an obvious link between our thoughts and how we feel.

The ability to perceive fifth-dimensional existence involves resolving the duality between being fully in your body and aware of your environment, while at the same time being connected to your higher self. From our higher self we can learn to observe our emotions and experiences while maintaining perspective. From this position of empowerment, we can make choices about our feelings and actions.

Living in the fifth dimension involves recognition that each and every thought that we have affects our reality, and the realities of those around us. While our individual power may be limited by our beliefs, our contribution to the mass consciousness alters the experience of our species. As each individual creates, the world is influenced. What we create is our choice. The outcome of experience is always affected by choice.

It takes discipline and awareness to successfully navigate through fifth dimensional reality. While we already have direct experience with our environment, understanding how our thoughts influence outcome is only the first step. Positive thinking must lead to positive feeling, or the conflicts in our vibration may lead to undesired outcomes. If fear or anger continuously enters your thoughts, your experiences reflect those emotions. The secret to truly influencing the world is to remain in a state of love, whatever the third dimension brings.

Transformation Exercises

1. Practice connecting to your higher self.

2. Sit quietly in a public place and glow with joy.

3. Understand the energy of each person who is drawn into your field.

Healing of Self

'The field of awareness organizes itself around our intentions.'

Deepak Chopra, 'The Way of the Wizard', 1995

Paradise Lost

He had it all, but it wasn't enough. He was a successful stockbroker, married with five children. Then, things started to go wrong. His business failed. His wife left him and took the children. He was alone.

He got involved with a new crowd. It was a crowd that thought deep thoughts and spoke deep words. They talked about life and art and expression and revealed to him everything that he had been missing. He soon found, however, that his friends were able to express themselves much more openly. He walked the streets an ex-stockbroker, while they were new to town. Old friends kept showing up, questioning him about his choices. He found life frustrating and desired more.

At age 42, Paul Gaugin left Paris on a ship bound for Tahiti. There, he began to paint bright, colorful pictures of Tahitian women and tropical landscapes. His paintings became famous and valuable. A contemporary of Van Gogh and Cezanne, Paul Gaugin is renowned for his influence as an artist.

Do you ever think about running away or changing your life? Where is your Tahiti? Sometimes it crosses my mind to go somewhere else, to start a new life in a new place. I have friends who have done this. While many people have left my city to live elsewhere, many others have made my city a destination of choice. It seems that the definition of an ideal place is different for everyone.

Uprooting would be a difficult decision for me. The roots of friendship are built through a lifetime and are something that I will not discard lightly. Perhaps the Internet is the tool to allow people to relocate and still maintain contact. Video conferencing is already available. Eventually, holographic projections will replace the phone call and people will have face-to-face conversations globally. The only problem is that you still can't hug holographically.

Suppose that you did decide to move to paradise. Would it be warm and sunny all of the time? Would there be an abundance of food and drink, beautiful people and ocean breeze? Would you relax on the beach for the rest of your life?

A few hundred years ago, before James Cook brought Western civilization to Tahiti, the Polynesians lived in paradise. They had everything they needed. The people were beautiful, tall and slim and bronze. They had nothing to worry about but their bliss.

It wasn't enough for them, either. The people of the area known as French Polynesia weren't satisfied in their paradise. They were bored. There were two major outcomes of this boredom: overpopulation and warfare.

I can understand how procreation could happen frequently in such a place. As the population grew, the paradise of the island was diminished by lack of privacy. Islanders packed their belongings in canoes and settled on other islands, each like the garden of Eden.

Imagine in your mind the beauty of this paradise. Clear blue water, white sandy beaches, and tall lush vegetation. Fruit grows abundantly, and you can easily catch fish just by throwing a net in the water. The air is warm and clothes are necessary only for adornment. Even the tropical storms are pleasant, as the rain is warm. You have everything you need for a life in paradise.

This paradise wasn't enough for the Polynesians. Soon, tribal warfare became common among the natives. Canoes full of painted warriors would travel across the seas to neighboring islands. They would steal and rape and kill. Even those who have everything want more.

Paul Gaugin did not have a happy ending in his trip to Paradise. He lived on the islands for two years, and then went back to France. He hated it again, and returned to the island of Hiva Oa, where he stayed until his death eight years later. During his final years, paradise failed him and he barely survived a suicide attempt a few years before his natural death.

Do you really think that running away will work? I think that contentment comes from within, wherever you are. Paradise can be found, but not in travel books.

Transformation Exercises

1. Describe the primary roles that you currently participate in.

2. Rate your level of satisfaction with each of the roles that you play.

3. List roles that you desire to add or enhance.

4. Describe an ideal setting for a vacation.

New Age Healing

WHAT IS HOLISTIC healing? Though this knowledge is now second nature to me, and certain circles of friends are highly informed, most people do not understand what it is all about.

There are many modalities of holistic healing. To classify my specialization, I am an energy healer, working both on and beyond the physical body. To be more specific, one of my healing sessions usually blends shiatsu, aromatherapy, reiki, reflexology and therapeutic touch. Though each of these techniques deserves extensive description, here I will only address generalities.

The current movement of society towards holistic healing is both a new discovery and a remembrance of old skills. Though technology has been introduced in some holistic modalities, most healing involves very old techniques. Healing with the hands has been practiced at least as long as recorded history and there is pictorial evidence of reflexology and massage in Ancient Egyptian art.

Healing is not curing, and once an illness has become manifest, it may require more than preventative practice. Healing is the act of becoming whole and at peace with oneself. Healing deals not only with the body, but also with the mind, emotions and spirit.

The main concept behind holistic healing is that it deals with the whole person, as opposed to one of our components. Standard medicine tends to look at illness or disease as separate from the individual and treats it as such. Someone with a bladder infection receives medication to fight the infection and fix the bladder. Holistic healing instead tries to determine what is occurring in the person's lifestyle that results in a bladder infection. While Western medicine can be effective and is often necessary, there is also a tendency to overlook the root causes of illness.

Holistic healing is preventative rather than reactive. Based on establishing a balanced lifestyle, and dealing with issues before they manifest physically, holistic healing becomes a way of life. Some take this to the extreme, changing their diet and exposure to environmental stress. Others simply raise their awareness of issues that may lead to distress and adjust accordingly.

A simple example for comparison is headaches. In standard medicine, the treatment of a headache usually involves drugs. Once the pain cycle has begun, a painkiller is administered so that feelings are numbed and pain goes away. I know one person whose headaches were so extreme and frequent that she had Botox injections in her scalp to deaden the nerve endings. Of course once the Botox wore off the headaches came back.

In contrast, holistic healing investigates the root cause of headaches. Are there stressful or emotional issues that lead to consistent neck and shoulder tension? Can these situations be alleviated, or can life be perceived as less stressful? In cases where headaches are persistent, massage and energy therapies are performed not on the head, where the pain is felt, but on the neck and shoulders, effectively reducing the tension that leads to the pain. A good backrub can often alleviate a headache.

Another key distinction between standard medicine and holistic healing is ownership. A medical doctor takes responsibility for your health and attempts to make you better. A holistic healer will state that only you can heal yourself. The healer doesn't heal. The healer only assists in the process. When one reads about remarkable recoveries, such as the remission of cancer, it is always the individual who healed him or her self. A true holistic healer would never claim responsibility for miracles.

As I discuss my personal development as a holistic healer, I realize that there is much more to it than simply learning how to help people feel better. My capabilities to heal have increased, but the personal transformation that I have undergone involves more than just knowledge and experience.

In becoming proficient at holistic healing, I have undergone my own healing, as does anyone involved in the field. In order to grow, we must recognize and address our own issues. I have experienced dramatic changes at all levels, including physical, mental, emotional, and spiritual. Once you begin the path of holistic healing, change and improvement are constant.

Transformation Exercises

1. Write an evaluation of your current physical health.

2. Write an evaluation of your current mental health.

3. Write an evaluation of your current emotional health.

4. Write an evaluation of your current spiritual health.

5. Identify how these four areas are connected within your current state of being.

No More Headaches

ALL PEOPLE EXPERIENCE pain. Some pain is a direct response to injury or disease. Some pain, such as headache or muscular tension, is a learned response to various stimuli. Though the pain from a learned response is real, it can be alleviated.

Years ago, I was a long time sufferer of migraine headaches. The severe peak of a headache would last for three or four hours. The headache hangover lasted until the next day, but at least it was tolerable. Then it would start all over again. I would have headaches daily for weeks at a time.

I was so afraid of the pain that even the slightest reminder of previous headaches would set me off again. My eyes would water and my sinuses would fill. I would feel a severe throbbing pain near my right temple. Any light seemed glaring and would often cause me to vomit. To cure myself, I would take painkillers, hide in a dark room and suffer until it went away.

I went to see doctors and had my eyes checked, did blood tests, and took other such measures. The net result was that there was nothing wrong with me, except for one thing. I was experiencing pain.

Many different things would trigger a headache. Studying for exams, problems at home, eating the wrong food. Sometimes, I would get a headache simply because I had read the word 'headache' in the newspaper. I apologize to any readers with the same affliction.

One pleasant day, things changed for me. I started feeling pain and realized that it had been months since my last attack. I immediately thought 'Wait a minute... I don't get headaches anymore'. Instead of increasing in intensity, the headache went away and didn't come back.

I realized how much of my headache had been a reaction to my expectations. Every headache that I had experienced had been extremely painful, so when one started I prepared myself for the worst. When my expectations changed, so did my headaches.

I also realized how much my lifestyle had changed, and how happy I was. I realized that previously stress was no longer with me. I realized that my entire attitude was different from when I was experiencing frequent headaches. Knowing that I was not ruled by headaches felt wonderful.

A year or so later, the headaches came back. Again, I would wake up in the middle of the night, head pounding in pain. I would take some pills and suffer for a couple of hours before getting back to sleep.

I started to analyze my situation. Why had the headaches returned? I realized that I was in the middle of some important decisions, and hadn't yet made up my mind. My headaches were the result of unresolved conflict. The conflict was causing stress, and the stress was leading to headaches.

People hold much of their stress in the muscles of the upper back, shoulders, neck and jaw. When muscular tension increases, the flow of blood and energy is impeded. There is usually a difference between where the pain is occurring and where the blockage is. Understanding this point is critical to alleviating headaches.

There are two aspects to ridding yourself of headaches. One occurs at the time of the headache. Another is the lifestyle that leads to the headache.

When the headache is occurring, try not to focus on the pain. Instead, focus on relaxing your muscle tension. Take deep breaths and stop thinking. Try to concentrate only on your breathing. Breath through your nostrils. If assistance is available, have someone rub your shoulders, neck and upper back. Have them use lots of pressure.

The second aspect of eliminating headaches takes place between headaches. Headaches do not occur without cause. Lifestyle, habits and emotions can all contribute to headaches. Feelings of conflict, doubt, fear or anxiety result in physical tension. As tension increases in your body, a headache may start. Massage can relax tense muscles, but if the stress remains, the tension returns. To rid yourself of headaches, you must address the conflicts that are creating tension.

Ridding yourself of headaches is not just a matter of willpower. It is a matter of recognizing and changing the patterns in your life that lead to headaches. Change your life and heal yourself.

Transformation Exercises

1. Describe your own patterns of headaches.

2. Book a massage.

3. If you do not experience headaches, identify any other problem areas of your body that may result from stress.

Natural Healing

As I PRACTICED Tai Chi in the park, a thought crossed my mind. How much of our stress and anxiety occurs when we are indoors? We all know that a refreshing walk in nature can calm the mind and reduce tension. What are the factors that cause this to be true?

When we are out in nature, we breathe fresh air. Sometimes it may not be clean, but it provides us with more oxygen than when we are inside. Even when we are sitting near an open window, much of the air we are breathing is stale. Outside is usually cooler, unless the air we are exposed to has been artificially conditioned. The air that we breathe, and how we breathe it, has a tremendous impact on our emotions and feelings.

When we are outside, we usually have more personal space. We find it easier to be grounded. Indoors, we are often working in groups, or closer to more people. Of course, being outside in a crowded area does not reduce stress. It is when we venture into the vastness of the world that we begin to see things through different eyes.

Indoors, we are often focused on some particular issue or task. We may be trying to resolve the matters at hand, or working on an intellectual problem. There is a greater tendency to use our mind instead of our body. If the task is not to our liking, or if we feel out of control, tension can develop. By going outside, we can leave our problems behind for a while. We live for the moment, as we hear calming sounds and see the beautiful scenery. Going outside allows us to shut down the mind chatter and begin to relax.

During guided meditation, we are often asked to picture a place of peace and tranquility. Whenever I have heard people describe their special place, it is always outdoors. They see themselves beside a lake, on a beach by the ocean, beneath trees in a forest, or in a meadow or oasis. When we picture a peaceful outdoor setting, it is rarely raining.

As you visualize our special environment we realize that nature is so invigorating because we are one with the earth. Though we see ourselves as unique individuals, we cannot avoid the influence that the energy of the earth has on our body. When we disconnect from nature and natural surroundings, we effectively reduce our link with our main source of energy.

Begin your healing process by venturing into the world. When you feel stressed or tense, go for a walk and allow yourself to reconnect. Often by getting away from the problems at hand, solutions are forthcoming. There is nothing more relaxing than sitting (or standing) with your back against a tree. Proximity to plants and trees and flowers not only supplies us with beauty, it allows us to share and absorb their healthy balancing energy.

I have spoken earlier about a Buddhist monk named Bhante who taught me to walk like a monk, slowly and deliberately. Instead of walking with the intent of getting somewhere, I learned to walk simply to enjoy the act. As I slowed down, I began to see more of the world around me. Things that I would have stepped over become more apparent in my awareness. By deciding that my walking wasn't just transportation, I reached places that I had never been before.

Whenever you feel depressed, stressed, anxious or tense, become aware of your surroundings. In all likelihood, you are indoors. Give yourself permission to heal, and make a point of getting out into nature. You may find lots of excuses not to take the break, but convince yourself that you will better deal with your life after you have begun the healing process. Go out into nature, and allow its beauty and power to help you balance.

Transformation Exercises

1. In meditation, visualize a place of peace and beauty.

2. Take a walk outside.

3. Sit by a tree.

Personal Healing

How CAN ONE die healed? It seems as if there is conflict in this statement. The conflict is not in the statement itself but in the definition of healing. In standard medical practice, healing deals specifically with the body. When a broken leg is healed, the patient can walk again. When cancer is healed, the patient does not die. To a medical doctor in the game of life, a death is a loss.

In holistic practices, healing is the act of becoming whole and at peace. Many people carry pain from incidents in their life. Bottled up anger and frustration can last for ten, twenty, even seventy years. A gray-haired man told me of anger at his parents over an incident that happened when he was eleven. A man nearing his seventies still feels hatred for his father who died almost thirty years prior. A woman in her forties is still affected by sexual harassment as a teenager. When we are hurt and our life is altered, we may carry the pain for the rest of our lives.

Many holistic healing therapies appear to work with only the physical body. The objective is to assist in the balancing of energy flow and to help release the blockages created by emotional issues. Feelings of stress, anxiety, fear and rejection first affect our flow of energy, and if they are not dealt with can manifest physically.

Healing involves understanding the emotions that have broken down your aura of health. Sometimes the issues have progressed beyond the point of physical healing, and while the spirit can realize freedom, the body cannot. Though our immediate desire is to cure the physical ailment, the most important goal is to feel the freedom of inner peace.

In breakthrough therapy, our personal issues are identified and investigated. Difficult as it may sound, true release arrives when we feel love and gratitude for our experiences. A traumatic incident may alter our viewpoint and improve our life. When we understand the effect the incident has on us, and realize that it was an important step in our spiritual growth, we find joy within ourselves.

Often, a traumatic incident results in blame, anger, or even hate. We hate the person that imposed their will and blame our pain and issues on someone else. We question why it happened to us. Quite often the feelings are true and the actions of another are unforgivable. To release, we do not need to forgive. We need to understand the impact of the incident on who we are, and how our life was changed. If you love yourself and who you are, then you can only be thankful for all the experiences that guided you to be that person.

Maintenance of anger, hate, or internal pain is a choice. To hate someone for something that happened years ago, while understandable, is still an emotion of your own making. A new perception can help you refocus. How did your feelings direct your life? What are the positive events that occurred to you as a result of those feelings? Did anger direct you to focus your energy on growth or success? Did fear allow you to empathize with others experiencing similar emotions? Did rejection cause you to seek acceptance from another direction? Each pain experienced alters your life path, and you must realize that many of your discoveries would not have occurred without the pain. Ultimately, forgiveness is a gift that you give yourself.

All humans die, and as we approach death, it is time to look back at life and understand it. Healing includes the realization that everything that happened to you was necessary. We progress when we understand why things happened, find joy from this understanding, and reach the peaceful feeling of acceptance and gratitude. Some people die still carrying their hate and anger, while others manage to release these emotions and feel whole. It is possible for a person to heal before they die. Understanding the transience of our physical existence and the continuance of spirit, it is really spirit that matters. Carry your peace and tranquility into death and the experience of your soul is expanded.

Transformation Exercises

1. Describe an incident in your life that you feel you will never get over.

2. Make a list of the problems this incident has caused in your life.

3. Make a list of the beneficial life changes that resulted from the incident.

4. Why was this experience necessary for your growth?

Give Peace a Chance

IT IS SO easy to be at peace. One must simply relax and breathe. Nothing matters but the moment. All thoughts of past history can be discarded, and saved for later contemplation. All hopes and fears and desires for the future can also be discarded, as things will come with time. What matters most to you now is who and what you are.

Choose to spend the next few moments at peace with yourself. Let your feet touch the floor, relax your shoulders, and breathe deeply. Put all thoughts aside, and just simply enjoy being you, now. Take a few moments and relax into balance.

When you come back to this writing, realize how much power you have over yourself and who you are. Moving out from your moment of peace, which direction do your thoughts take you? Does the peaceful feeling remain, or are other thoughts changing your vibration?

There are many things that invade our peaceful moments. Concerns and worries, hate and anger, fear and doubt. Many of these thoughts are triggered by external sources, though ultimately all issues come from within. However, for the moment all thoughts are irrelevant and can be put aside. In honor of your soul, take what you deserve...a moment of peace. The world can be changed and it begins with you.

Transformation Exercises

1. Enjoy a moment of peace.

2. Practice moving into a vibration of balance and peace.

3. Teach the skill to others.

Healing of Others

'The meeting of two personalities is like the contact of two chemical substances: if there is any reaction, both are transformed.'

C.G.Jung

The Healing Touch

IN A STUDY at McMaster University in Ontario, Canada, Dr. Stephen Sagar proved that the hands of energy healers have electromagnetic fields 1000 times stronger than those of average people. Healers are doing something unique. The heat that we generate from our hands is a skill that most people don't have. We all have the ability to heal with the hands, but only some of us will choose to develop the skill.

I first realized my healing hands capabilities when I took a course in shiatsu massage. Each week in class we would learn about the structure of the body, and then observe, practice, and experience the massage techniques. Working with a volunteer patient, I began to discover an awareness of the energy in her body. Rather than trying to work intellectually, which I normally do, I allowed myself to work intuitively. When I found an area of resistance, I pushed at it until I felt the resistance go away.

When I achieved my first level of Reiki, I discovered the ability to generate heat from my hands. The heat had been there before, but now it was even more evident. When I worked on someone, I felt that my hands were like radiators. When I worked on many people consecutively, my hands were really hot, and the top of my head was almost steaming. I was effectively channeling energy.

Practicing Therapeutic Touch taught me to change my intention. Rather than trying to give someone a boost of energy, I learned to offer energy for the patient to take. Instead of 'giving them a boost', I allow them to 'soak up energy like a sponge'. No matter how hard I work as a healer, I cannot heal a patient who does not desire to heal. My responsibility is to be clear, open, and grounded. It is the patient's responsibility to heal.

There were a number of changes that I experienced as my healing capabilities progressed. I learned to meditate, and how to shut down the mind chatter. I learned how to relax and focus and live in the moment. I began to see others not as physical beings alone, but as beautiful beings of energy, a soul projecting a body.

As I began to understand the workings of the body from an energetic perspective, my healing capabilities accelerated. My learning and skills advanced continuously. I discovered that intention is our most powerful tool. Intend to be a healer and you will be. Intend to transfer energy and you shall. Intend to heal yourself and you shall heal.

A key principal in healing is to touch without expectation. Learning to touch someone else without intention of reward is critical to healing. It is also necessary to see the other as an equal deserving respect and love. The healer cannot let ego take over the healing session. The healer is simply a conduit and must adjust to that perception.

Learning to be a healer has required formal education, training, practice, reading, discussion, self-analysis and growth. Healing requires an adjustment of spirit, the ability to be humble and to observe your self objectively. Not everyone will be willing to pay the dues to become a certified healer, but everyone can activate innate healing abilities.

There are many people who have learned to heal with their hands and many people who have not. Those who can heal are not physically different from those who can't, though their physical capabilities are enhanced. This implies to me that energy healing is something that can be learned. Do healers have an innate ability, or have we simply learned how to influence energy?

Evolution is occurring through intent and self-discovery. We have always had these capabilities and now we are allowing them to surface. Our next stage of evolution is not only physical but also intellectual. Learning to influence our own energy field, and those of others, is a milestone event for mankind.

Everyone has the potential to heal. The first step is to learn how to touch. Give someone a shoulder rub or foot massage. You don't have to be a certified expert to help someone feel better. Just remember to move slowly and use gentle firm pressure. There is much to learn about energy healing, but all progress starts with you.

Transformation Exercises

1. Hold your hands one inch apart, palm facing palm. Describe the feeling.

2. Hold one hand over the other, palm over the back of the other hand. Move one hand closer and further away from the other, without touching hands. Are you sensitive to the temperature difference?

3. Do some research on Reiki, Therapeutic Touch, Qi Gong, Falun Gong, or any other energy healing technique.

Energy Healing

MANY OF THE holistic healing practices require comprehension of a basic concept. The body is perceived not as a structure of solid matter but as a focused field of flowing energy. Our energy field has a tremendous influence on our health and the healing process.

The energy field is often identified as the aura, which is a multi-layered glow surrounding the body. Energy flows through the body along pathways called meridian lines. These lines, and major meridian points, can be seen on a chart of the body, such as those used by an acupuncturist.

When your aura is vibrant and flowing smoothly, there are no health issues. When your energy flow is weakened or impeded in some way, your health declines. All discomfort is associated with imbalances or blockages in the energy flow. The intent of healing is to assist the patient in opening channels and balancing the energy.

From the gentleness of Therapeutic Touch and Reiki to the aggressive healing of Shiatsu and Chiropractic, there are many holistic therapies that work with energy. Each of the practices is uniquely different, and each is appropriate in different situations. Each has different intent and methodology. Reflexology, Acupuncture, Ear Candling, and Qi Gong are other healing practices that affect the energy field.

In most cases, issues in the energy field become apparent well before they are manifested physically. If the issue can be resolved before physical manifestation, standard medical assistance is not required. In this manner, holistic healing practices can be preventative in nature.

What causes imbalances in the energy field? In some cases, traumatic injury or illness has a sudden impact on a person. In these cases, standard medical attention is required. In many other cases, energy is blocked due to emotional pain or social conditioning. How one feels about oneself has a direct influence on energy flow.

Conscious or sub-conscious memories can also be retained within the energy field, and eventually they manifest into physical issues. For example, people who regularly have headaches usually get them the same way each time. Certain muscles are trained to react to stress. Tension in these muscles can lead to headaches. The next time you begin to feel stressed, be aware of how your body is reacting.

When you become aware of your own energy field, self-healing takes a different approach. Identification of energy blockages, and the habits that lead to those blockages, begins a process of allowing energy to balance. For any healing to take place, the intent of self-healing must be present.

In standard medical practice, the doctor is asked to cure. In holistic healing, it is not the responsibility of the healer to fix the patient. The healer is only there to assist. Ownership of healing must remain with the patient. The only person who can balance your energy flow is you. Of course, it is often easier to balance with assistance. Meditation can help tense shoulders, but a back rub makes relaxation easier.

We are reminded regularly that our health care system is in a shambles. Hospitals close, nurses migrate, patients in need are turned away, or left to sleep in hallways. Many of the cases that end up in the hospital could have been prevented. If people regularly experienced energy healing, illness would decline.

The way to alleviate issues with the health care system is for all people to learn energy healing and to take care of themselves. Balance your own energy and your health will improve. Help your friends and family before they get sick and a trip to the hospital may not be required. If someone has gone too far, and you are visiting them in the hospital, don't just sit there and chat. Take hold of their ankles and help them to ground and heal. You can still chat, but at least be connected.

While energy healing has been part of humanity for thousands of years, our progress in medical science has led us away from these core concepts. Society has a tendency to blame issues on external influences (it's not my fault), and look for someone else to make things better. A return to a society where all members learn and practice energy and touch healing will make our civilized world healthier, happier, and more enlightened.

Transformation Exercises

1. Evaluate your own energy field. Where are your issues?

2. What is the source of the issue?

3. Seek balance.

Monkey Do

IN BUSINESS MANAGEMENT training, whenever someone has an issue that needs to be resolved, it can be termed as a 'monkey on the back'. It is usually something that requires attention and effort and will not go away without being dealt with.

Often, people come to their manager and try to give away their monkey. They may indicate they are looking for sympathy or advice, but are actually attempting to give away ownership of the problem. If they are successful, they will leave their manager's office and the monkey remains behind. If the manager offers to take care of the problem, the attempt has been successful. Even if the problem has been reassigned to someone else, the original owner has fulfilled his desire to be rid of the issue.

The problem with accepting monkeys is that they begin to pile up. One staff member leaves and before the issue is dealt with, another person comes in with a different monkey. Soon, the manager has a barrel full of monkeys and is unable to get anything accomplished. The manager's own tasks are postponed to deal with the problems inherited from others.

The trick to efficient management is to ensure that anyone bringing a monkey into your office takes it out with them. A manager can sympathize, advise, offer solutions, or suggest a pathway. However, an effective manager must always decline ownership of the majority of issues. Even on the telephone, it is better to provide a solution before you hang up than to accept another task. In most cases, the person with the monkey will accept guidance once they know that you will not relieve them of their issue.

Enthusiastic rookies are usually the first to step in and offer an easy way out. 'No problem, leave it with me and I will take care of it'. An experienced manager will instead say 'Here is what you need to do to resolve the issue'. The rookies will keep on taking ownership of problems until they burn out, at which point they either leave management or learn how to say no. An experienced manager spends the day shortening task lists, not increasing them.

The same concept applies to holistic healers. It is critical in the role of the healer to not take ownership of another's issues. Though empathy may lead us towards acceptance of someone else's problem, it is not the healer that heals. The healer can only assist in the process, helping guide the recipient towards a state of balance. If the subject refuses to heal, there is nothing that the healer can do about it.

Our own personal power is challenged when we try to fix someone else's problem. Not only have we taken on the responsibility for something that is really out of our control, we have also allowed our subject to alleviate their own responsibility. By becoming the person who will fix the problem, you also become the object of blame if things don't work out. How many times have you heard someone speak about a doctor or healer who 'wasn't any good' because they did not resolve a health issue?

Reverting ownership to the person with the issue is a discipline that can be learned. However, when we are emotionally attached to someone with health issues, we are more likely to take those issues into our own lives. It is difficult not to worry when someone you care about is ill or injured. A friend of mine is currently suffering from stress related issues. This is not surprising since both her mother and daughter have recently experience medical issues. Concern for the welfare of others often creates an imbalance within us.

It is difficult to be a healer and not get involved. We want others to stop suffering, to get better, to see the gaps in their lives that have led to their problems. It is frustrating when you want to help someone and they do not want to be helped. It is so much easier to identify causality in the lives of others than it is to see your own shortcomings. What is important to remember is that accepting another's monkey is entirely your choice.

Transformation Exercises

1. Make a list of the monkeys that people have given to you in the past week.

2. Make a list of the monkeys that you have given away in the past week.

3. Become aware of giving or receiving a monkey, and then make the appropriate choice.

Safe Energy Healing

WHILE RECENTLY WORKING with a group of healers, I heard someone comment about bad energy. He stated that he had picked up some bad energy during a healing session and that he had not protected himself properly. I have heard other healers talk about protecting themselves and to some it is common practice. I believe differently.

In my view, each of us is entirely in control of our own energy field. While outside influences are constantly striving for attention, it is always our decision to choose where our focus goes. Our energy field resonates with our thoughts, both consciously and subconsciously. If we choose to believe bad energy can attach to us, then it will be so. However, power is ours to keep or give as we decide.

When an energy healer creates a protective barrier, there are direct effects on the capabilities of the healer. Firstly, healing power is diminished, as the healer weakens the energy exchange with conflicting thoughts of love and fear. Secondly, the recipient is aware of the shield and feels the healer creating separation. By believing in bad energy, we give it power. By setting up a protective shield, we create the potential of battle.

Instead of generating protective barriers, I choose to enter all healing interactions openly. I am confident with my energy field and know that no one can harm me energetically. While I regularly pick up disharmonious energy from those that I work on, my own energy field is so vibrant that the disturbing energy simply melts and fades away. I remain aware of energetic disturbances, and when I identify an issue, I simply direct my entire field to rebalance. It is possible to eliminate the power of disharmonious energy by setting your energy field to absorb and dissipate any harmful energy.

The primary role of a healer is self-healing; to balance and activate ones own energy field so that healing powers are increased. When a healer grows in spirit, the benefits affect many. When a healer overcomes fear of intruding energy, the true healer emerges.

Transformation Exercises

1. Describe a situation where you picked up illness or bad feelings from someone else?

2. What was your own state of being at the time?

3. Describe a situation where you were exposed to someone who was ill or depressed, yet remained happy and healthy.

4. How were you different in the two circumstances?

A Team of Angels

To MANY PEOPLE, the concept of healing occurs primarily at the physical level. Seeing man as a machine, medical professionals address disease and injury primarily at a physical level. Their work is important, and my father is alive today because of the proficiency of the medical professionals who successfully replaced his aortic valve. This surgery has added years to his lifespan.

As my father prepared for surgery, my awareness of energy healing revealed that there was a lot more going on. While I allowed the medical staff to take over the physical requirements of my father, I chose to participate in his energetic healing. When any healer is presented with a subject, healing powers are increased due to empathy and energetic interaction. I discovered that when the catalyst was someone of great importance to me, my healing powers were amplified.

While my father was in surgery, I visualized him on the operating table. I moved into meditative state and set the intention of surrounding his body with an egg-shaped sphere of energy. In my mind, the egg formed well, and the energy that I perceived was strong and steady. Then, I realized that the egg would be strong without me and recognized that there was energetic support assisting in the process. I looked deeper and perceived that there were seven spiritual entities channeling energy into the egg around my father.

I perceived the entities as spiritual forces, human in shape, but without legs. They were yellow-white in color and each had two arms extending into the shell of the egg. Instead of legs I visualized something like a comet trail extending from the waist. Three forms stood at each side of my father and one was positioned above his head. Whether these forms were angels, entities, or simply my imagination, they were helping to maintain a healing field around my father.

Later, when I entered the recovery room to be with my father, I moved into healer vibration and then held his feet. Acting as a grounding rod, my energy encouraged his to reconnect with the planetary vibration. As this connection was completed, I perceived that there were two entities positioned at his shoulders. Together we formed a triangle, and the energy circuit was completed.

There are always many stories and many ways to perceive any situation. This story is my perception and one that I choose to accept. While I did not perceive the spiritual entities visually, I felt that they were there. Imagine the feeling of standing in a dark room and knowing that someone is there even though you cannot see them. Whether you choose to believe this story or not is up to you, but for me it is just another reminder that there is more.

Transformation Exercises

1. Describe an experience where you have helped someone heal.

2. Describe an experience where someone has helped you heal.

Powerful Reflections

A COMMON SPEAKER'S story tells of a dog that walked into a house full of mirrors. Seeing the many eyes staring back at him, the dog growled, and a thousand dogs growled back at him. Another dog entered the house, and seeing all the other dogs, wagged his tail in delight. A thousand dogs wagged back, making him even happier.

A friend told me about a spiritual group that he attends regularly. Each month, after discussion and meditation, the group is given an assignment that encourages spiritual growth. One month, the assignment was to choose 'the biggest a**hole in your life', and to go out of your way to be nice and do friendly things for him/her. Obviously, the intention was to begin changing the current relationship.

However, when I heard of the assignment, I realized it would be impossible for me to complete. As I thought through all of the people that I know, there was not one that I would consider an 'a**hole'. Of course there are some people whose company I prefer over others, and some people whose philosophy is different than mine. While others may do or say things that push my buttons or awaken opportunities for anger, I choose to see them as unique souls walking the path of life.

When we define someone as an 'a**hole', we give them power. We blame our anger or frustration on them and allow them to influence our lives. Often, people spend inordinate amounts of time thinking about the other person and how they can get even. There is a tendency to see them as inferior or threatening, or to think that our lives would be easier without that person around.

I choose a different path. If someone pushes my buttons, I attempt to identify why those buttons are easy to push. What is going on within me that allows a simple comment to raise my anger, or my doubts, or my level of frustration? If someone's opinion can cause anger in me, why am I so sure that my way is the only way? There are always many different ways to look at an issue, and the more certain I am that mine is the only way, the more likely that my perceptions are confused. There is always another way and there is really no opinion that is absolutely correct.

It is not always easy to defer emotions. Sometimes my choice to not become involved in petty interactions causes others to question my emotional capability. However, I recognize that many emotions are a choice. I choose not to waste my time or energy dwelling on someone else's opinions. I have my beliefs, and live with them. My life becomes easier when I allow others to have their own beliefs rather than opposing them.

Of course, like all humans, I do react to certain stimuli. It is not always easy to avoid anger, or to prevent reaction to statements or actions that I disagree with. Conversely, sometimes it is essential to react if you truly believe in your values. However, by assigning the term of 'a**hole' to someone else, you have given away your power, and your energy is drained. If you can recognize that everyone else is another soul on the journey of life, your own experiences become simpler and easier.

Transformation Exercises

1. Identify three people whose company you find challenging.

2. What are the characteristics that annoy you?

3. List three situations where you have shown the same characteristics.

It's Up to Them

I WAS SPEAKING with friend about his job, and some of the difficulties he was facing. As he described the situation and conflicts, I recognized some steps that could help. I suggested some changes that my friend could make and he responded immediately 'But they are the ones who need to change!' Immediately, I saw the truth and broke out into a grin. 'Isn't that statement the source of most human issues?'

The division between 'us and them' often leads to conflict, or disagreement, or hostility, or blame shifting. When we perceive someone as different, we may assign judgment to those differences. Our judgments often delegate differences as threatening or non-threatening. When we perceive someone as different, we may see their beliefs as ridiculous and write them off. When we perceive someone as an opponent, we give them energy and power. The more that we strengthen barriers because of differences, the more difficult the opposition becomes.

Imagine two extreme contrasts. In one world, every individual is completely alone, disconnected from everyone, and fully responsible for his own peace of mind. In the other world, each person shares in a common energy, connected to all, and yet is still an individual. In the world where we are alone, every person is a separate entity. Each person has different effects on us, beginning at neutral and moving towards either extreme. We like or dislike others based on our feelings and beliefs and how they compliment our own ego.

The existence of ego is necessary to our survival as individuals. Without ego, we do not recognize ourselves as special or different. When we begin to feel challenged or threatened or upset, it is usually ego that is speaking. Our need to be recognized as important often leads us to speak up even when listening would be a wiser choice.

To overcome issues of conflict, begin to look at the other person in a neutral manner, then attempt to perceive elements that are common between you. Notice similarities rather than differences. Notice elements of power, skill or knowledge that add to your own being, and enhance the energy of the world. See how the other is both a reflection of you and a beautiful addition to the harmony of the planet.

It is not easy to learn new perceptions. When we are particularly challenged by the efforts or character of another, it can be difficult to accept them. Anger often builds and others may act as catalysts driving you towards action or change. However, it is important to remember that the easiest way to overcome 'us and them' is to form a common 'us'. When we expand our group and perceive commonalities, conflicts can be reduced.

Transformation Exercises

1. Identify two people you know who have disagreements.

2. List the reasons why each person could be right.

3. List the reasons why each person could be wrong.

4. Identify how the characteristics of each allow the disagreement to continue or escalate.

Death

'The warrior neither seeks nor flees from death.'

Dan Millman
Way of the Peaceful Warrior, 1980

The Funeral Poem

If I should die in summer,
The gardens will be sown.
My hyacinths and daffodils
Will grow up on their own.

If I should die in autumn
The leaves will cover me
I lie in restful peacefulness
Beneath the maple tree

If I should die in winter
The frost will keep me fresh
For winter is renewal
And we are not of flesh

If I should die in springtime
The earth shall bury me
And fertilize the flowers
Beneath the maple tree

The White Room

Picture yourself sitting alone in a white room. The room is filled with bright white light, though you cannot see any lamps or light bulbs. The ceiling is white, the walls are white, and the floor is white. There is a door to the room, but it is locked. Imagine yourself in this room, and answer the following question: How do you feel? Before you continue reading, close your eyes and formulate an answer.

Your answer may surprise you, because how you feel about being alone in the white room can indicate how you feel about death. Are you afraid of death, or do you feel peaceful about the end of your physical existence?

Though some people are comfortable with the thought of death, a fear of death is common. Whether it about our self or of someone close to us, death is something over which we have little control. Fear of death can be considered in three different areas: fear of the circumstance of death, fear of loss of existence, and fear of losing others.

A friend of mine was in a very serious car accident. The car rolled over a few times, and he smashed his head against the steering wheel. Pulled unconscious from the car and rushed to the hospital, he survived and recuperated fully within weeks. Later, I was speaking to him about my fear of the experience of death. My friend commented that if he had died in the accident instead of just being knocked unconscious, it wouldn't have felt any worse. Anticipation of pain is often worse than the pain itself.

We have all experienced pain. Some, if not most of us, have experienced excruciating pain, and dealt with it. Can the pain of death be any greater than the pain of life? My grandmother, speaking from her deathbed, said 'All the pain doesn't matter now. What matters to me is family and seeing all of you here.' What mattered was her comfort with the fulfillment of life purpose. If we approach death content with the path that we have led, pain will be overcome.

Fear of death can also be a fear of non-existence. What will the world be like without my unique presence? If you were to die next week, are you satisfied with your accomplishments? If not, get yourself on track. Live each day as if it were your last. If there are relationships that need healing, don't wait before making the attempt to communicate. If there are tasks that you wish to accomplish before you die, get started.

There will always be more things to do than you are capable of including in your lifetime. Life is full of never-ending possibilities and it is only through prioritization that we finish the things that really matter to us. If you fear death because it may prevent you from achieving certain dreams, then it is time to start manifesting those dreams now.

Losing a friend or loved one can be our most difficult experience. We become so connected to those that we love that we cannot imagine going on without them. Often worries about others supercede worries about ourselves. It is important to realize that most of this fear is self-generated. Why worry about someone not being around if they are still here? And as many people have discovered, when a loved one dies, life does go on. It is a matter of choice whether we grieve for the rest of our lives, or find joy and appreciation of the actual time that we had together.

I have no concerns about the length of my life. I choose to live each day in joy and fulfillment. I have already made peace with family and friends and have expressed my love for them. Death will come when it is meant to come and I shall not choose to live my life anticipating the unknown. My philosophy of death arises from my firm belief that there is continuance. I see death not as finality but as a graduation, a completion of one chapter and progress to the next. Life is a beautiful gift and something that we can choose to use wisely. Death may bring an end to this particular game, but the soul is eternal.

Transformation Exercises

1. How did you feel in the White Room?

2. What are your fears about death?

3. If you have seen a dead body, describe how you felt at the time.

4. What do you believe happens after death?

The Eulogy: Speak from the Heart

THERE COMES A time in many people's lives when we are asked to deliver a eulogy. In most cases, this occurs because we were close to the deceased. We are dealing with our own emotions as well as those of the deceased's family and friends. Many are asking 'why?' and now we are expected to give the answer. What in the world do we say?

I recently was put in this exact position. My cousin died unexpectedly at age thirty-nine. His body just stopped working when a blood clot blocked his main artery. I was shocked when I heard the news, as are most people when they hear similar news.

Given the responsibility of preparing a eulogy, I determined my objectives. A eulogy can be developed which will make everyone cry. There is a distinct possibility that this may happen and provide the release needed by those who remain. However, I believe a eulogy is meant to comfort and encourage the living. You have the opportunity to give the audience something to take with them as they leave the memorial service.

As I prepared the eulogy, I set five objectives:

Let the Audience Know the Person

Every person is unique, and every death is unique. For the audience members who didn't know the deceased very well, it is important to tell something about the person.

What is it that made this person special? If he was caring and giving, don't just tell us, show us. Relay an anecdote about something the person did that proved his or her compassion. Likewise, if the person showed strength in a particular situation, tell us the story and let us conclude the obvious. A good eulogy should make the audience aware of the person's character and this is best achieved through anecdotes.

The anecdotes must be chosen with care. It is appropriate to tell a story that makes the audience laugh. It is inappropriate to tell a story which focuses on particular weaknesses of the deceased. Nobody leads a perfect life and the audience is usually well aware of the deceased person's faults. They don't need you to remind them. Instead, tell a story that reveals positive character aspects.

Address the Needs of the Audience

Though a funeral or memorial service is centered on the deceased, it is really held for the living. Your audience needs help, and you can provide it. You must first recognize the pain suffered by the audience and the loss that they have experienced. Express sympathy to those closest to the deceased and to those who have traveled a distance to pay their respects.

Most of us don't like dealing with death. It brings out our insecurities, our feelings of guilt, and our perception of mortality. When delivering a eulogy you have the opportunity to philosophize about life and death. While any single death is disturbing, it is an end we shall all experience. You can help the audience deal with this circumstance.

Uplift the Audience

The people in attendance are vulnerable. They want you to say something meaningful and are listening intently. Take advantage of this opportunity to help improve your audience's outlook on life.

Determine the Lessons Offered by the Deceased

When someone dies, we often ask the question 'Why?' Usually, there is no answer. We tend to look at a person's life in comparison to the lives of others. We identify what was lacking in a person's life and wish our friend or family member would have had more time to realize his or her dreams. We may wish we had treated the person differently, or we find comfort in the relationship that existed. All of these issues are really related to us, not to the deceased. Any feelings of guilt or judgment are created within ourselves, and only we can choose to release these feelings and move on.

In any life, lessons are learned and examples set. Search for these and share them with the audience. How can you use the deceased's life as an inspiration? What challenges did the deceased face and how did he or she choose to address them?

Use Appropriate Mannerisms

The atmosphere when delivering a eulogy is not appropriate for many of the common elements of speaking. Vocal variety can be used well, particularly in the volume and tone of voice. While the eulogy requires a somber tone, it is appropriate to use humor, particularly amusing anecdotes that summarize the person's character in a positive way. Always deliver a eulogy from the heart and it will be successful.

Transformational Exercises

1. Make a list of five people who have passed on. They may be people you know, or public figures.

2. What aspects of each of their lives can be seen as inspirational? If the answer is none, keep looking.

3. What lessons have you learned from each of these people?

4. If you mourn for a parent or loved one, write a eulogy even if they have been gone for years.

The Last Leaf

IMAGINE BEING A leaf. You quickly grow to full size, and then spend the rest of your life in glorious greenness, waving in the breeze and soaking up the sun and the rain. Then a change occurs. You start to age. Your color begins to change. Around you, all of your friends are aging too. As far as your eyes can see, your whole species begins to radiate orange and gold and red. One by one, you see each leaf fall to the ground, dead.

They lie there decaying into brown. Thousands and thousands of dead, as far as the eye can see. You are surrounded by death and carnage and destruction. Other leaves lie scattered across the ground, heaped and layered, exposed to the elements. They no longer feel the energy of life. They simply lie there and decompose. Is there any way that you can escape the same fate?

The time has come. You are alone on a branch, withered and brittle. A gust of wind breaks your connection with the life-giving tree and you flutter to the ground to rot. Your existence is complete.

The last leaf doesn't know about spring. The leaf doesn't know about the cycle of life and how in a few months the temperature will rise and all of the trees will begin to sprout new leaves. The leaf doesn't know that this has gone on for generations - birth, life, aging, death, and rebirth. Having experienced only one spring and one fall, there is no certainty that anything exists beyond the completeness of the cycle. But it does.

What do you believe about rebirth? Do you think that there is more to come, or do you believe that it all just ends? After death, is there consciousness or just a black void? Is there awareness or nothingness? I suspect that we will find out one day, one at a time or in a group. We won't grasp the truth until we have been there.

In the meantime, how does your belief affect your life? Are you afraid of death? Does it cross your mind regularly or not at all? Do you lead your life as if death walks close behind you, or as if you have an eternity to get things done? How do you feel about the end of your physical existence?

To believe in something for which there is no proof requires faith. Faith requires belief in the unknown. Faith requires letting go of logic and allowing a belief in something for which there is no logic.

Throughout our lives, we use logic to protect us, to resolve our issues, to provide for ourselves. We anticipate causality. We think sequentially. We have expectation of results. Our minds analyze and look for ways to explain things. Problem solving becomes a way of life.

What are the consequences of foregoing logic? In many circumstances, the consequences are harmful. Foregoing logic in the management of your finances can lead to some surprising bills. Not thinking logically in a time of emergency can be dangerous.

What are the consequences of believing in after-life?

If you believe and it is true, you will excitedly move through the stages of your life.

If you believe, and it isn't true, you will never know.

If you don't believe, and there is no after-life, then you won't know that you were right.

If you don't believe and it is true, you didn't get the benefit of faith in your life.

What is the benefit in faith? I can live life with joy. I can see the stages in my life with pleasure and understanding. I can anticipate without fear. This is my belief and I share it with you. It may not be your belief and that is fine. Only you are in charge of your belief system. Me, I take a gamble. I look at the consequences of having faith and also at the benefits. Faith wins.

Are you a gambler? Before you roll the dice, remember:

Even the last leaf doesn't know about spring.

Transformation Exercises

1. Take a walk in the woods or in a park.

2. Consider the cycle of life.

3. Sit or stand with your back against a tree and feel its energy.

4. Bring home a leaf.

The Flowers that Opened My Eyes

I DON'T REMEMBER many funerals before that of my paternal grandmother. Though she was the last of my grandparents to go, she was the only one I had known as an adult. I was twenty-seven years old when she died.

Nana had been ill and had spent a lot of time in and out of hospitals over her final five years. She had cancer and piece-by-piece the doctors took her apart. She did have stamina and each time after surgery she would recuperate, travel, and see family and friends around the world. Then she would get sick again and come home for more surgery.

Towards the end, Nana became an advisor to me. Through her own pain she could see the pain in my life. I was very confused and lost, and very depressed. I was struggling for direction in my life. Though I eventually found the answers within myself, Nana was a catalyst in helping me turn things around.

The last time I spoke at length with Nana, we talked about life. She said that despite all of the pain and all of the heartache in life, it was worth it. She also said that the cars, the house and the luxuries in her life didn't matter in the end. What mattered was family and having people close to her.

Soon after, Nana was back at the hospital, and we held a birthday party for her. All of the family was there, including aunts and uncles and cousins. We crowded into the room and sang 'Happy Birthday' as we presented Nana with a cake. She was seventy-five. I gave her a hug and a kiss, but we didn't talk much that day. That was the last time that I saw her alive.

A few days later I was at my grandmother's funeral. My parents and I were standing by the open casket. I was looking at my grandmother for the last time. The base of the casket was covered with dozens of flowers, large chrysanthemums with many white petals. Suddenly, out of the corner of my eye, I saw motion. I turned my head, and looked at the bouquet. One of the flowers started to move. As it vibrated, first one petal fell off, and then another, and then another. It was like a Walt Disney movie where the flower grows really fast. I watched in amazement as every petal fell off of the one flower. None of the other flowers moved, just that one.

I went downstairs with my mother, and only when we were alone did I mention to her what I had seen. She asked me to show her and we went back to the casket. Sure enough, there was one bare stem among dozens of flowers with a small pile of white petals beneath it. My vision was confirmed.

This was something that could not happen. I cannot invent a physical explanation for what I observed. But I do have a metaphysical explanation. My dead grandmother was communicating with me. What is metaphysics? It is the belief in a reality beyond what is perceptible to the senses. Well, I cannot perceive in this reality anything that would have caused that solitary flower to shed its petals.

I struggled to understand the message. What did it mean? What information was my grandmother trying to pass along? I tried to figure out what she was communicating. My family had experienced some difficult times over the past few years and I imagined that the petals were teardrops.

Finally, I have come to a different understanding. I have been learning and growing, understanding more about myself and my existence; exploring my spiritual side and trying to understand my mortality. Then it came to me. I understood the message. It is simple message. It is a wonderful message.

There is more.

There is more to our existence than we understand. More than science or technology can explain. More than anything that we can perceive within our physical limitations.

There is more.

Transformation Exercises

1. If you have had a metaphysical experience, describe it.

2. How did this experience affect your life?

3. Do you remember a specific funeral? What were your feelings at the time? How many of those feelings do you still carry with you?

4. Identify if your feelings are related to yourself rather than the deceased.

Evolution

'Always listen to experts.
They'll tell you what can't be done, and why.
Then do it.'

Robert Heinlein

The Next Phase

IF HUMANITY IS to survive, it is necessary for us to evolve beyond our current condition. While most people believe in the concept of evolution, many believe that it only occurs in the past. We see ourselves at the top level and cannot imagine more. Just as a caterpillar cannot understand butterflies, humanity cannot foresee what we shall become.

We are reaching a point of critical mass and the next step is upon us. We will not fully understand the transformation of humanity until it has already occurred. In order for humanity to evolve, each individual must evolve. Though there will always be trailblazers and nay-sayers, the real jump in humanity occurs when the majority achieve enlightenment. Whether this enlightenment occurs at a physical, intellectual or spiritual level remains to be seen.

Individuals are in charge of their own self-growth. While it may seem defeating to look at the world and its problems, most of what we think is going on is influenced by the media. As each person looks at their immediate environment, we realize that our experience is directly related to our beliefs and actions. As we make personal changes, the people around us are influenced. As each person is influenced, the world begins to change.

Despite the history of mankind, the world will not be improved through force. Our world becomes better through trust and love and compromise. It changes when enough people connect to the mass consciousness and decide to be at peace. It takes place when we realize that each soul is unique and special, therefore no-one is. The distinction involves recognition and respect of each person's unique energy, while removing hierarchical judgments of superiority and inferiority. We must be both teacher and student with everyone we meet and feel no threat moving between roles.

The challenge that many face is freedom to grow within their environment. Many of us face intolerance or derision or attack. Many people meet quietly and secretly to share ideas and enlightenment.

Around the world there are more rules than ever before and part of our challenge is to show others that freedom of belief and expression is not threatening. The secret is that there is more than one way. As long as each person accepts that another may think differently, we grow as a species. Together we compromise and create paradise.

We must learn to express love rather than anger, joy rather than sorrow. We must learn to express compassion and understanding, especially when faced with differences. We must learn to live with our own strength while empowering others. We must feel excitement about learning new and different ways. We must learn to share our own viewpoints without expectations. Ultimately we must accept that every person is special and deserves to be treated that way.

The energy of humanity is changing. As each person raises consciousness, we move one step closer to mass awakening. As each person discovers enlightenment, the joy is passed on. Each time you experience a moment of peace, the vibration of our universe moves towards calmness. Evolution begins within, and it starts with you.

Transformation Exercises

1. Describe the freedoms and restrictions in your immediate environment.

2. Describe the freedoms and restrictions in your country.

3. Describe the freedoms and restrictions in the world.

4. Choose the level of freedom reflected in your vibration.

The Leading Edge of Thought

THROUGHOUT HISTORY, PHILOSOPHERS have asked deep questions about who we are and what we should do. The answers change over time. While some directives keep repeating, other times brand new answers stimulate a leap in the human condition.

When Abraham Lincoln proclaimed freedom for all regardless of color, the human condition advanced. This is not to say that suffering was alleviated, but for the first time there was recognition of the equality of souls. The color of a person's skin should not affect freedom of choice.

When Mahatma Gandhi demonstrated a way to create change without violence, he showed that resolute determination and true love of others could lead to a better world. It is important to stand up for your rights, but it is equally as important to let others stand as well.

When Albert Einstein proclaimed that E=mc2, the application of his thoughts were turned into atomic bombs and nuclear power. He also opened the door to an understanding of quantum reality that we are only beginning to perceive. As science and knowledge progress, so does the human condition.

What will be the next breakthrough in our perception? Will it be the recognition of auras and the acceptance of ourselves as beings of energy? Will it be the revelation of undiscovered power as we learn to manipulate our universe through thought alone? Will we uncover hidden secrets that reveal the truth about the origins of life on this planet? Or will we finally be introduced to entities and a community beyond our planet earth?

We now have the potential for another leap in consciousness, another advancement of the human condition. It involves the discovery of ourselves and the recognition that the attainment of personal enlightenment is the most perfect goal. The experience of enlightenment is different for each person. We each move through stages of growth without ever running out of places to go. Enlightenment is a continuous journey, not a finite destination.

As we approach enlightenment, we realize that our thoughts directly influence our world. What we see, what we hear, how we think and how we live are all within our control. The workings of our mind have tremendous influence on our momentary existence. It is possible to rule your thoughts instead of having your thoughts rule you.

Recognition of feelings is important, as our intuitive capabilities have increased. In addition, many people are discovering innate telepathic and empathic skills. It is possible to pick up a lot of information in a short period of time by being aware of someone's energy field and evaluating body language. Communication is not limited to verbal output. It is important to listen not only to what is said but also how it is said. The energy of speech can be as important as the words used.

As we look back at the development of humanity, it becomes apparent that what we know to be true is only real until new ideas come along. While it may be difficult to imagine a breakthrough in the current state of the human condition, I believe that it is only a matter of time before we recognize that humanity has grown again.

Transformation Exercises

1. What breakthroughs have you seen in your life?

2. What breakthroughs do you anticipate in the next ten years?

3. What breakthroughs would you really like to experience?

Continuance...

As YOU MAY have discovered by now, the journey of self-growth is endless. We can continually work on improving within, and at the same time alter the world that we experience. By always respecting others and holding the intention of continuous self-improvement, we each make a positive contribution to the energy of our planet.

As we advance our personal vibration, the benefits are felt within and without. As masses succumb to the peace and beauty that is here for our enjoyment, we begin to create the paradise that we have always desired. Paradise does not involve everyone being the same, or everybody lying around in peaceful bliss. Instead, paradise involves the joy of living and being unique, of leading the creation of your own life.

For some paradise involves exercise and exhilaration, sweat and satisfaction. For others, the same paradise is defined as the lone creativity of an artist, or the motivation of group energy to complete a project. We each have in front of us a world of resources and opportunity. All we need to do is use it. By moving ourselves forward and creating a positive light for self, the rest of the world comes along.

We each play a small role. Together we change our world.

For the most recent writings and material, please visit my web site:

www.glennstewartcoles.com